D0752457

ALIENATION

Dealing With The Basic Problem Of Man

Author

Carroll Thompson

CTM Publishing
P.O. Box 763954
Dallas, Texas, 75376-3954

ALIENATION:

Dealing With The Basic Problem Of Man

CTM Publishing
P.O. Box 763954
Dallas, Texas, 75376-3954

Scripture quotations are all taken from the <u>New American Standard Bible</u>.

ISBN# 1-879655-02-0

Dedicated to

Thomas Parnell Mahoney

A godly man
who has followed the Lord
with all his heart.

CONTENTS

PREFACE

In the following chapters the subject of alienation is pursued in three areas: man separated from God, man separated from man, and man separated from himself. The scope of man's problems are covered as we follow man through the phases of alienation. We will see the changes of behavior beginning in the Garden, and follow these behavior patterns found in Adam and his descendents. These patterns are found in men today. Some of these you will recognize in yourself. I will be sharing from over twenty years of ministry in these areas. The practical as well as the theoretical will be brought forth in simple, understandable, Biblical language. I believe many will find healing and freedom as they read the pages of this book. The Spirit of God will be present in His Word as a two-edged sword to cut and to heal. Do not be afraid to allow the Spirit of God to enter into the depths of your being. The purpose of the book is to bring healing and freedom to every person who reads it.

I suggest you turn to the back of the book after reading each chapter and follow the steps of practical application for that chapter. This can be a meaningful experience for you. Perhaps a home study group could join you in discussion and prayer as you work through these truths.

Chapter One

Society in Trouble

In the past the Innuit people of the Artic region have fascinated us due to their ability to live in frozen waste land. With no outside support they have managed with the meager resources of their environment to survive the most difficult circumstances of the cold. They sustained their families in isolation. Constantly moving, constantly seeking food sources, they overcame the most desolate region of snow and ice in the world.

When the government moved the people into villages and domesticated them, many no longer could cope with life. In one community of 1500 persons, researchers found that every adult had contemplated suicide, every second person had attempted it in one form or another, and nearly one-quarter of the population had tried to commit suicide in the previous year alone. Ninety-five percent of the adults suffered from alcoholism, and ten percent of the children were sniffers of gasoline.

What went wrong with these invincible people of the North? What happened when they were isolated from their culture? Sustained by government subsidies they no longer had to struggle for survival. The government provided housing, schools, and health care. Yet most of these people experienced despair and hopelessness that led to self-destructive behavior.

They had become aliens within another culture, and something within them had died.

The same problem of despair and hopelessness is a phenomenon of the twentieth century. People have become alienated within their own culture. Problems of depression and loneliness, and a sense of futility and emptiness, have caused many of this generation to turn to drugs and look to suicide as a way to escape. Many find themselves lost in isolation and nothingness. They have become alienated within their culture.

An example of these modern-day aliens is the gangs that rule in the inner city areas. They form alien groups that attack and destroy existing communities. Attributing all their pain to the present culture, they attack and destroy in order to be free. Violence becomes the way to break out. Rioting, stealing, and burning, they lash out against a culture that has filled them with pain. The inner cities of this nation are also filled with drugs and depravity, both being clear evidence of alienation within our own society.

Alienation is not just a problem of the poor, but it has entered into the midst of wealth and affluence. With opportunities that surpass everything in the history of man, with technology that brings all manner of entertainment, comfort, and security, a generation has turned from normal life patterns. Drug abuse, immorality, violence, and suicide indicate a generation has lost its way. What has happened to cause this tragic state?

Isolation of the human soul is the deepest pain man can experience. In isolation he experiences alienation, which is the pain of death. Drug abuse, sexual exploitation, and suicide are signs of a generation trying to break out of alienation. Drug addiction is a way to escape from the pain within. The theme of death is foremost in much of the music of the day; symbols of death on clothing express a hopelessness about life. What has brought a modern generation to this point of despair?

All life support structures have deteriorated within our society. The termites have invaded the building and destroyed much of the substructure. Basically there are three substructures of society: family, church, and civil government. These three furnish a protective covering in which life grows. One could describe them as a cocoon which the larvae of an insect spins in order to protect itself during the pupa stage. Life is fragile; it must be protected.

The deterioration of the family has exposed a whole generation to alienation. Divorce and broken relationships have broken the cocoon of the family. Someone has said that during the 1950s, seven out of ten families were normal with two original parents; now, it is estimated that the inverse is true, seven out of ten families do not have the original parents. When divorce comes the cocoon breaks. An undeveloped individual is exposed to a crisis he emotionally is not ready to face. Fear and insecurity come in upon him; he assumes responsibility for the failure; and life becomes a painful experience of loss, disappointment, and rejection. The door is opened for alienation.

The need for community and union is deep within man. The breakdown of community within and outside the church has left many in isolation. Nothing is more painful than to feel isolated in the midst of people. Rather than being a healing body, the church has become, to a great extent, an organization living for itself. Decline in church attendance reveals that the usual church no longer is relevant as a support structure in society. Much of society no longer relates to God as a personal Being concerned about their welfare. Ministers have disappointed and exploited people, and have driven them away. The individual has lost another layer of protection from the cocoon, and faces life without purpose and meaning. He considers God, who has always been the strength of those going through a crisis, remote and unconcerned; then alienation comes in on his human soul. The person is alone.

The isolation continues as society loses faith in its institutions. The trust and confidence in governing officals is at a low level. Cynicism has come in. The Watergate scandal has left a nation distrusting. With the increase of complex problems in society, government is facing problems far beyond anything in the past. These problems come when the public's confidence in the government is the lowest. The law enforcement structure and judicial system are under great pressure to perform and maintain order during a time of violence, crime, and racial conflict. The courts and prisons are overflowing with social violators. Insecurity and unemployment in the job market speak of radical changes companies have initiated without a social contract with their workers. Statiticians have estimated that one-half of the job force will be temporary by the year 2000. Many conflicting groups, clamoring for their rights, have brought turmoil in the land. Moral issues, conflict between racial groups, feminism struggling with the male image, speak of a society struggling to identify itself. This lack of identity and cohesion speak of a social structure breaking down. Hopelessness and isolation fill the soul of the individual. Without the protective covering of righteous government the individual feels exposed and insecure about the world in which he lives.

When a person feels exposed and naked, fear and anxiety come upon him. This anxiety drives him into further isolation. Fearful of the outside world, he builds walls of protection. These walls can be high and thick, difficult to break through. Inside is an insecure individual, alienated from society. In alienation he becomes introverted and self-oriented. Seeking entertainment to fill his emptiness, reality is lost. Life becomes a vicarious experience within an entertainment world. Perhaps he wants to take hold of life, but fear keeps him from becoming involved. He chooses the painless way of non-commitment. Isolation can reach the point that one takes on a survival mode of living for the moment, clutching, grasping, and clinging to anything and everything that indulges the soul and satisfies the flesh. Life then loses all purpose and meaning. Eventually death becomes the contemplated way to escape the pain of emptiness. Alienation has finished its course. It always ends in death.

Alienation is more than a problem of society; it is a problem within man himself. It is here that the book will focus. We will look at alienation from three perspectives: man separated from God, man separated from man, and man separated from himself. Here we shall see the full working of alienation in all aspects of man's being.

Chapter Two

Guilt, Shame, and Fear

A young woman came out of the psychiatric hospital tormented by guilt and shame. Slash marks upon her wrists showed how deep the guilt was. Thoughts of suicide constantly barraged her mind. Over three years in the hospital did not take away the pain. The guilt lay so deep she had been unable to admit to herself the cause of her guilt. She had suffered deep depression since the beginning of puberty. Why was she tormented so much? What did she refuse to remember?

Guilt, shame, and fear are the first works of death, coming out of alienation. All of this began in the Garden when man was separated from God. "And the Lord God commanded the man, saying, 'From any tree of the garden you may eat freely; but from the tree of the knowledge of good and evil you shall not eat, for in the day that you eat from it you shall surely die'" (Genesis 2:16,17). Man's transgression brought death. The death man experienced was alienation, and man's behavior changed immediately.

Until that day man had been free; he did not know fear. He was free to draw near to God, free to fellowship with another without embarrassment, free to communicate his most intimate feelings and thoughts, free to come near in relationship without being self-conscious, free to be himself without fear of rejection. Until the day man experienced the death of alienation, he was free from fear.

The day man transgressed and broke covenant with God, he became a hiding, covering creature. "Then the eyes of both of them were opened, and they knew that they were naked; and they sewed fig leaves together and made themselves loin coverings. And they heard the sound of the Lord God walking in the garden in the cool of the day, and the man and his wife hid themselves from the presence of the Lord God among the trees of the garden. Then the Lord God called to the man, and said to him, 'Where are you?' And he said, 'I heard the sound of Thee in the garden and I was afraid because I was naked; so I hid myself '" (Genesis 3:7-10).

These three statements express the immediate effect of alienation upon man: "I was afraid...I was naked...I hid myself." For the first time man experienced guilt, shame, and fear. His first response was to distance himself and cover. Here we see the beginning of isolation. No longer able to be transparent, fearful of being too close, man has behaved by hiding and covering himself ever since.

The Pattern of Guilt

Following the pattern of the first man who put the blame upon the woman, men still try to maintain innocence through denial and blame. First, a form of denial comes through minimizing an act or by ignoring consequences. A man tries to convince himself that the act is not that bad after all; it is normal. He sets forth all his intentions as being good. He rejects norms that would disapprove of his behavior. He brings forth a new order to give more freedom. Second, he lays the blame on another. Adam blamed the woman, and the woman blamed the serpent. Man refuses to accept responsibility; at any cost he must maintain his innocence. By denial and blame the natural man handles his guilt.

Accepting the responsibility of guilt brings man to a process of comparison. The focus of attention is upon others. Finding sin in others helps to alleviate his own guilt. A mental process of constant comparison issues forth. He is not looking for good, but for sin and failure in others. Every discovery causes him to feel better about himself. So the search continues.

Then there is the mental process of balancing the moral ledger. For every credit there must be a debit; the books must balance. If he can do enough good to balance the bad, the conscience finds rest. So he is constantly looking for some way to do good. It is a process of removing guilt by one's own righteousness.

Guilt is more than a mental or psychological problem. It has deep spiritual roots. It involves the problem of evil. The day he experienced the death of alienation, man also experienced the entrance of evil. The effect of evil upon the soul of man goes beyond the perception of mind or the response of emotions.

What does evil do to the soul of man? First, evil destroyed innocence, "their eyes were opened." When he lost innocence, man experienced a sense of nakedness. This awareness of self came with a sense of shame. It caused an immediate reaction of covering himself and hiding. Shame then became a basic problem for man. Some of the deepest roots of shame and guilt come from experiencing evil in the time of innocence. This problem is not evident at first in children, but the fruit of shame and guilt will come out later.

The young woman in the beginning of this chapter was carrying deep feelings of guilt, shame, and fear. She had refused to remember that her father had sexually abused her when she was four years of age. When she reached puberty, she was unable to accept her body's developing into the body of a woman. Everything about herself took on the concept of guilt and shame. Yet inside she was driven with certain sexual impulses that frightened her, that she could not deny. Being driven with sexual desires and filled with guilt, she found herself in a dilema with which she could not cope. Withdrawing into herself, she became alienated from family and friends.

Second, when it comes in, evil defiles the conscience of man. He begins to feel dirty, and to see himself as unclean. He is experiencing guilt. The behavior of hiding and covering becomes compulsive. Ritualistic cleansing and washing, dressing immaculately, and obsessive cleanliness in the house indicate a neurotic reaction to guilt. Along with this comes the projection of guilt and blame on others. Impending judgment waits for all who fail to measure up to his self imposed standards.

If he does not project it on others he will internalize the guilt. Self-punishment, self-hatred, and self-accusatory thoughts bring one to consider suicide. The young woman mentioned in the beginning of the chapter lived at this point for several years. The torment of guilt gives no peace. Alienation always brings death in some way.

Dealing With Nakedness

Man in his attempt to deal with guilt makes a choice, either to cover himself with a religious covering or to accept nakedness as normal. Returning to nakedness for some is a way to recover innocence, but innocence once lost can never be recovered. For the sinner righteousness is based upon truth rather than innocence. No matter how innocent man tries to make his sin, the result is always the same: guilt and shame.

Most men choose a religious covering for their nakedness. For this reason the roots of every culture are found in its religion. The word "culture" has the basic meaning of "cult or religion." The nature of man as a sinner is to cover himself with a religious covering. How does one recognize a religious covering? What is it that makes up the fig leaf covering for man's nakedness?

The first thing about a fig leaf covering is its intense adherence to the letter of the law. Generally by one's interpretation of that law he sews together a suitable garment. Righteousness becomes a display of one's goodness; his works are put before the eyes of the public. This intense commitment to religious order accompanies spiritual pride, devoid of compassion for the sinner. A righteousness that separates him from the world, refuses to hear its cry for help. His religion consists of much sacrifice to God, but no mercy for the sinner. Jesus spoke to the religious leaders of His day, "But go and learn what this means, 'I desire compassion, and not sacrifice'" (Matthew 9:13).

Legalism, spiritual pride, and ritualistic washings make up the religion of this man. Yet underneath these coverings he hides behaviors both sinister and deceptive that lack the true character of righteousness. That which man sews together to make a covering does not take away his sin or guilt; the sin remains, the uncleanness remains. Seclusive and performance oriented, he makes his sacrifice to God. He has become a hypocrite. Thus most religion falls into disrepute, and the world questions the motivation of religious people.

Guilt will drive a man into fanaticism. The warning comes from the Scriptures, "If you remove the yoke from your midst, the pointing of the finger, and speaking wickedness, and if you give yourself to the hungry, and satisfy the desire of the afflicted, then your light will rise in darkness, and your gloom will become like midday" (Isaiah 58:8,9). Guilt will place a heavy religious yoke upon man. Under this yoke he will point a critical finger at all others, and out of his mouth will come words of judgment condemning all who do not accept his yoke.

Free From Guilt

Religion does not remove the guilt of man. Guilt will remain until there is cleansing and forgiveness of sin. In the Old Covenant people made three offerings for sin: the sin offering, the guilt offering, and the peace offering. They offered the first for the actual sin, the second for the guilt of the trespass, and the third an offering of thanksgiving that the past had been laid aside. Being free of guilt requires that one deal with his sin in all three ways.

Until one acknowledges sin guilt will remain. Confession exposes sin; we must face sin. The Scripture describes this transparency as "walking in the light" (I John 1:7; Ephesians 5:8). We must establish truth about sin before man and God. Covering sin allows sin to remain. Uncovering sin allows truth to bring man to repentance and forgiveness. Hear the words, "If we confess our sins, He is faithful and righteous to forgive us our sins and to cleanse us from all unrighteousness" (I John 1:9).

Obtaining forgiveness is only a part of man's salvation, as there is also cleansing from all sin. Then God removes all defilement of sin, and man is actually free from sin and guilt. At this point man finds peace. The cleansing agent on earth that cleanses man from sin is the blood of Jesus Christ. "How much more will the blood of Christ, who through the eternal Spirit offered Himself without blemish to God, cleanse your conscience from dead works to serve the living God" (Hebrews 9:14).

Until God cleanses his conscience, a man cannot be free from guilt. God must remove not only sin, but the defilement of it. Through forgiveness God lifts the weight of his sin; through cleansing He takes away the defilement of his sin. Only then is he free. Read the prayer of David in Psalm 51, and let this be your prayer.

What He cleanses, God also covers. God provides a covering of righteousness once man allows his nakedness to be exposed. "I will rejoice greatly in the Lord, my soul will exult in my God; for He has clothed me with garments of salvation, He has wrapped me with a robe of righteousness" (Isaiah 61:10). God covers only that which He cleanses.

Chapter Three

Hostility

Historical grudges that create a cycle of hatred and vengeance have alienated nation from nation and have separated ethnic groups within nations. The ongoing conflict among the Croatians, Serbians, and Muslims in Yugoslavia is a present example of alienation. Locked in a death struggle, tens of thousands of people have died and millions have been made refugees. Armies are raping and pillaging, bombing and destroying. The innocent have become the victims of a most brutal attempt in ethnic cleansing. Once these were one Slavic people. In the sixth century they migrated from north of the Danube into what became Yugoslavia. For hundreds of years the terms Serb and Croat had only a geographical meaning. To this day they all speak the same Slavic tongue. Yet over the centuries geography, religion, and wars empires have waged to control this land, gradually split the people apart. A cataclysm of war now divides a small nation into three violent forces. Alienation has brought death to this land.

Why is man hostile toward man? Why has war dominated man's history? The story goes all the way back to the Garden where we find hostility and violence in the first family. The first son born to man entered into conflict with his brother and killed him. In this story of the first family, perhaps we can learn some valuable insights about alienation.

23

And the Lord had regard for Abel and for his offering; but for Cain and for his offering He had no regard. So Cain became very angry and his countenance fell. 'If you do well, will not your countenance be lifted up? And if you do not do well, sin is crouching at the door; and its desire is for you, but you must master it'. And Cain told Abel his brother. And it came about when they were in the field, that Cain rose up against Abel his brother and killed him (Genesis 4:4,5).

We saw man separated from God in the first stage of alienation; man's behavior became hiding and covering himself. Now at the second stage of alienation we find man separated from man. At this point we can see alienation working through hostility, man against man. Since the time of the fall, hostility as a basic behavior has dominated man's history. Conflict and division, anger and hatred, conquering and subduing describe this behavior. Why has he not been able to live in peace?

Without Peace

First, man has looked upon his brother as a competitor. When competition becomes the issue, elimination becomes the goal. Cain looked upon his brother as one competing with him. A selfish intent controlled Cain's thinking; somehow he must excel over his brother. There was not room for both of them. Since his brother excelled and found favor, he saw his brother standing in his way. Some way the brother had to be eliminated so that he alone would stand before God. What Cain failed to understand was that with God the issue was obedience; with Cain the issue was competition.

In reaction to his failure, Cain's countenance fell and he was filled with anger. Anger is that reaction of man that refuses to be put down, that determines to have what it wants, that causes a man to enter into conflict. Like a fire within, it burns until man is filled with hostility. It turns toward another with blame for the pain or loss experienced. Anger refuses to accept responsibility; blame holds the other person responsible. Finally, it bursts forth like an explosion with one intent, to destroy. Unreasonable, unpredictable is the anger that works in hostility.

Rejected Brotherhood

Second, man has no peace because he has rejected brotherhood. Anger has turned into hatred, and the full expression of alienation has come forth. Hatred is the rejection of brotherhood. Man has replaced all natural desire for community and union by a choice to live alone. He chooses to live without his brother, and in doing so he chooses to live for himself only. Man thinks this arrangement will solve all his problems, but at this point he enters into another phase of alienation, which is isolation. We will deal with isolation in a future chapter. Now we wish to dwell upon the basic concept of alienation as it works through hatred.

Webster defines hatred as a great dislike or strong aversion. However, when one places hatred with alienation, one sees enmity, division and hostility. Hatred now takes on an aggressive attitude which is more than malevolence. Separation comes first, then conflict. Hatred always destroys brotherhood through conflict and division.

Man no longer is a loving, communicating, fellowshiping creature. He stands as it were with spear and shield ready for battle. He has lost the concept of brotherhood; alienation within makes him believe that everyone is a potential enemy. Fear does not allow him to trust. Conflict and division fill his life. He lives without peace, without security, without love. Through conflict, pain, and fear, he learns to hate. Through hatred, alienation possesses his soul and he lives in isolation. Brotherhood is lost.

God provokes Cain with the question, "Where is Abel your brother?" (Genesis 4:9). Cain reveals the alienation of his heart when he answers, "I do not know. Am I my brother's keeper?" By viewing his brother as a competitor and refusing to be responsible for his welfare, Cain had rejected brotherhood. Man has lived in conflict ever since. "Now the deeds of the flesh are...enmities, strife, jealousy, outbursts of anger, disputes, dissensions, factions" (Galatians 5:19,20). Alienation has separated man from man.

Man has a basic need for community. Whether it be from the need of security or for union, man was not created to dwell alone. Here is the source of his deepest pain and fear. Brotherhood is a basic need within man because God created him in His own image. Within God there is no alienation. It is here that the mystery of the Trinity lies. There is such union that Jesus described it as, "...Even as Thou, Father, art in Me, and I in Thee, that they also may be in Us..." (John 17:21). In God is no division, no separation, no alienation. Man was created to live in that union of love with God and man. Here lies the key to wholeness.

A Call to Love

"For this is the message which you have heard from the beginning, that we should love one another; not as Cain, who was of the evil one, and slew his brother....We know that we have passed out of death into life, because we love the brethren. He who does not love abides in death" (I John 3:11,12,14).

The principle is very clear, "...he who does not love abides in death." In other words, he who does not love still abides in alienation. We have seen from the preceding paragraphs how alienation works death through division and hostility. Within man alienation is expressed through hatred which is the opposite of love. Death is in hatred, life is in love. To continue in alienation is to continue in death.

The call to love is the call to life. "We know that we have passed out of death into life, because we love the brethren..." (I John 3:14). Here one experiences a great transition from death to life. How can one be free from the alienation of death so deep within man's soul? God has provided the way. "And although you were formerly alienated and hostile in mind, engaged in evil deeds, yet He [Jesus] has now reconciled you in His fleshly body through death, in order to present you before Him holy and blameless and beyond reproach" (Colossians 1:21,22). Jesus Christ suffered the hostility and alienation of man working through hatred; it all focused at the Cross. It is He that can bring you out of death into life.

A Call to Union

When all lay down the weapons of hostility, we will have restored brotherhood. Man must again come into union with his brother and become his brother's keeper. Only then can there be peace on earth. For this purpose Jesus came, and for this He prayed, "[Father] may they all be one...that the world may believe that Thou didst send Me...I in them, and Thou in Me, that they may be perfected in unity..." (John 17:21,23). That which Cain rejected, Jesus Christ restores to man: unity and brotherhood. He breaks down the walls of hostility; only then does man come into union. As he comes into union, man comes into life. Those who refuse union are called the wicked,

"But the wicked are like the tossing sea, for it cannot be quiet, and its waters toss up refuse and mud. 'There is no peace,' says my God, 'for the wicked'" (Isaiah 57:20,21). Hear the entreaty of the apostle:

> I, therefore, the prisoner of the Lord entreat you to walk in a manner worthy of the calling with which you have been called, with all humility and gentleness, with patience, showing forbearance to one another in love, being diligent to preserve the unity of the Spirit in the bond of peace. There is one body and one Spirit, just as also you were called in one hope of your calling; one Lord, one faith, one baptism, one God and Father of all who is over all and through all and in all (Ephesians 4:1-6).

Chapter Four

Bitterness and Unforgiveness

Khieu Sam Phon, a ruler of Cambodia, was responsible for the death of 1.4 million of his own people in this century. Most of the deaths occurred through forcing the people to leave their homes and to go into the country without provision of food or shelter. Most died of starvation and exposure. His army killed all the professional people that could have maintained the society. This man demonstrated brutality time and time again. An unforgettable example took place when his soldiers took young, teenage girls and buried them feet down with only their heads above the ground. The soldiers then began to mutilate them with their bayonets. What would cause a man so brutally to kill his own people?

The rest of the story is that as a young boy, Khieu Sam Phon went to a boarding school where the other boys rejected him. It seems he was the brunt of much teasing and abuse. He did not experience the acceptance and fraternity of his peers. He was not hostile and aggressive; rather, he was subdued and passive. He held the pain inside; he did not express it in anger or hostility. He suffered alone; it seemed he had no friends. As a young man he was sexually impotent; no young woman filled the void in his life. One day when he was older and became a ruler, all the pain held inside came out like the fire of a volcano and destroyed his people.

29

Pain

Pain that is suppressed will come out in destructive ways: anger and hostility, blame and criticism, rebellion and violence. Time does not cause it to go away. It has a way of building up deep within the soul until it comes out in bursts of anger and rage. It looks for an object upon which it can vent itself. The trigger of release may be insignificant; the reaction can be extreme. Suppression does not diminish the pain, but pain remains and builds up pressure.

Pain held inside can create conditions of chronic sadness and depression, fear and isolation, self-punishment and suicide, addictions and addictive behavior. The passing of time does not diminish the pain, which remains covered and attached to the mind and emotions. If pain is too strong, one may go into denial and block it out. Yet the pain remains and will continue to bring about self-destructive behavior.

Unfortunately, man experiences many woundings and bruisings in his development. Children can go through terrible experiences in the home or in school. Abuse generates abuse, and violence creates violence because of the pain that remains. Children are vulnerable and the innocent become the victims.

Even as adults, people suffer many tragic experiences of loss and disappointment. Deep woundings of the soul take place in broken relationships, death, loss of health, loss of income and career, loss of family, et cetera. Events of life can be crushing; the pain can go very deep. Life can take cruel turns and leave a person bleeding on the roadside.

The pain grows deeper when one feels God has abandoned him. Many struggle with the question, Where is God when it hurts? Some feel God wills tragedies. After all, is He not all powerful, is He not in control? Why did He let a tragedy happen? The pain grows deeper and deeper as one sees God being responsible for what happened. On the other hand, God may seem remote and uncaring during a time of loss. In many cases, one does not experience His comfort, but only the memory of pain. Seeming abandonment by God at the time of pain may cause one to alienate himself further from God. The pain becomes more intense when one suffers alone.

Bitterness

What shall I say? For He has spoken to me, and He Himself has done it; I shall wander about all my years because of the bitterness of my soul. O Lord, by these things men live; and in all these is the life of my spirit; O restore me to health, and let me live! Lo, for my own welfare I had great bitterness; it is Thou who hast kept my soul from the pit of nothingness (Isaiah 38:15-17).

King Hezekiah was facing death in the middle of his life. He expresses the pain of his loss by saying, "Lo, for my own welfare I had great bitterness..." The lives of many can repeat this over and over. Is God the source of their pain? Is He responsible for all the suffering in the world? Many have grown bitter toward God because of their pain.

God is not the author of evil. The evil that destroys is in the world. Since the fall of man, a principle of evil has penetrated all the physical universe, bringing death and corruption. Man in his physical body is subject to the same law of corruption. The sin of man has brought death; death is in the world, sickness is in the world, pain is in the world.

Evil has penetrated man, making him the source of much pain as he exploits others to fulfill his own lust and greed. Much wreckage is left in his path as he lives for himself: he abandons wife and children; he tramples down the weak; he victimizes the innocent. The world is filled with pain.

Evil is more than a principle, a kingdom embodies evil. One needs to be aware of the strategy of the enemy: through bruises (pain) he binds and establishes control; destructive behavior takes over; sin comes in; and the flesh rules. This is bondage, this is slavery. The intent of God through the extension of His kingdom is "...to set at liberty them that are bruised" (Luke 4:18 KJV).

Out of a wounded spirit destructive behavior comes forth. What is more destructive than bitterness? Bitterness is a root that grows deep within the soul, and whose fruit is death. It is the cancer of the soul. From it all life dries up, activity ceases, isolation comes, weakness and depression prevail, all peace goes, the grace of God is cut off, the process of death sets in. Hear the Scriptures:

> Therefore, strengthen the hands that are weak and the knees that are feeble, and make straight paths for your feet, so that the limb which is lame may not be put out of joint, but rather be healed. Pursue peace with all men...See to it that no one comes short of the grace of God; that no root of bitterness springing up causes trouble, and by it many be defiled (Hebrews 12:12-15).

Forgiveness

Forgiveness is the key to releasing pain and receiving healing. A principle of the Kingdom is found in Luke 6:37, "...Pardon and you shall be pardoned." The literal meaning of pardon is "release." "Release and you shall be released." The principle is this: if you release the one who has hurt you, God will release you from the hurt. The term release gives the literal meaning of forgiveness. When you forgive you release the person and wipe out the debt. In forgiving you release God to work in you and the other person's life. On the other hand, unforgiveness binds you to the person that hurt you, you are bound to the past, and the hand of God is bound from working in that situation. Nothing can change. The pain remains.

Chapter Five

Isolation

What happens to people in isolation? Some of the most isolated people in the world were the Australian aboriginals. How they arrived in this land no one knows. Scholars have thought they lived on this continent more than 10,000 years. In all this time they never built a house, planted a seed, nor made clothes for themselves. They wandered across this large, barren continent, constantly moving, sleeping on the ground with the dogs, living off whatever nature provided. They called no place home. Afflicted with sexual diseases, bound by fear to the spirits of the land, their lives were not a Garden-of-Eden experience. They remind us that nakedness does not bring innocence. For thousands of years these people wandered in isolation without change except for the worse. How could they survive?

Their most primitive lifestyle speaks of a degenerative culture brought about by a mental strangulation that allowed no development of tools and techniques that would change their way of life. Note, they did make weapons. Here one sees the sad condition of men who lose themselves in alienation. They became wanderers without destination, vagrants without purpose. They entered a survival mode of existence. Actually they were no better than the animals. Alienation always leads down, not up, as the evolutionists would have us believe. These modern-day Cains, illustrate well what happens to people in isolation.

What did Cain do in isolation? (Read the account in Genesis 4:11-16.) When he rejected brotherhood, he became a wanderer and vagrant in the earth. He could nowhere be at rest for he dwelt in the land of Nod, the land of restlessness. In his isolation he cried out that his punishment was too great to bear. Man is a social creature for whom solitary confinement is punishment. He who killed his brother now must live outside the community of man. Along with the isolation came fear. Now he was afraid of anyone coming near him, afraid someone would kill him. Anyone that penetrated his isolation he considered an enemy, and he looked upon the approach of anyone as aggression. Here is the sad state of man, isolated and yet afraid for anyone to come near.

In the account of Cain one notices two things man confronts in his isolation: fear and restlessness. Why was man so restless? How could life be so empty? Was he not free to do whatever he wished? There was no law to restrain him, no one in authority to tell him what to do; he was free to do as he pleased. He did not have to work; he was responsible for no one. Had not isolation given him the freedom he had always wanted? He could come and go as he pleased. He could now live for himself. Why be bothered about anyone else? He did not need anyone; he would return to nature and live off the land. Perhaps he could recover his innocence by taking off his clothes. If he could only return to the Garden, everything would be innocent and good as it was in the beginning.

When Man Rejects Brotherhood

When he refused to be his brother's keeper, Cain entered into isolation. Here the terrible truth of isolation came upon him and he cried out, "My punishment is too great to bear!" What was Cain experiencing? It was not the happiness and freedom perhaps he had expected. He found that to be a wanderer was very painful. For the first time man experienced futility.

Cain experienced the futility of isolation. The Creator had said, "It is not good for man to be alone." Man was created in the image of God Who is a personal Being and whose nature is to love, have fellowship, and communicate. The union in the Godhead is so close He is called One God. The human mind has difficulty comprehending this truth. Yet man's soul cries out for union. There is an undeniable need for love, fellowship, and communication with another person. Isolation denies man the basic need for union.

Without union life is empty and man experiences the deepest pain. Nothing is more painful than emptiness. Much of his wandering comes trying to fill this emptiness. Surely somewhere, something will fill the hole inside. Perhaps no driving force is stronger in man's life than the emptiness of the soul. Here he has to deal with spaciousness and emptiness in life. Man remains a wanderer as long as he lives without union.

Futility grows within man when he discovers that to be without union is to be without purpose in life. Can there be greater futility for man than to live without purpose? Man experiences purposelessness as a wanderer. He is here, but why is he here? This question separates man from the rest of the animals. An animal would never ask itself this question. The line that has separated man from the rest of the animals does not seem to be there now. Man has become a wanderer without destiny. Is he any better than the rest of the animals? Is life in itself enough?

The terrible truth now comes crashing in upon Cain. Without brotherhood there is no purpose in life. The very thing Cain rejected has now robbed him of the meaning of life. A wanderer does not have purpose nor destiny. The emptiness of isolation came upon him in a most painful way and he cried out, "My punishment is too great to bear!" Life has become meaningless and empty.

The futility continues to grow. Man has lost union, he has lost destiny, and now he discovers he has lost identity. If man has separated himself from man, if man now lives without purpose, what makes him different from the rest of the animals? Man has reached the point that he has lost his identity. He begins to ask himself the question, Who am I? Most men spend a life-time trying to answer this question along with another, Why am I here? These are the two most important questions confronting man. In them are the meaning of life itself and the worth of the individual. Distinction, uniqueness, and worth all make up a person's identity. A wanderer does not know who he is or why he is here. He has lost union, purpose, and even himself. He wanders in futility.

One comes to see the frightening results of alienation. In isolation man loses perspective. Man does not find himself by looking within himself; neither does he find purpose by living for himself. When he no longer can see the face of God, man loses all perspective. Alienation carries one into a downward spiral of lostness and separation. The evolutionary view of the upward progression of man is not accurate. The contrary is seen in the case of the Australian aboriginal. In isolation there is retrogression. Man fulfills no purpose; there is no sense of destiny; he becomes like the rest of the animals. Man has been separated from himself.

Modern-Day Wanderers

Job describes a generation living in isolation. The scenario of a people living in a wilderness describes the emotional and spiritual conditions of a generation alienated from itself. The conditions are sad, the pain is real, the desolation is unbeliev-able. Get a mental picture of those who live in isolation.

> They are driven from the community;
> They shout against them as against a thief,
> So that they dwell in dreadful valleys,
> In holes of the earth and of the rocks.
> Among the bushes they cry out;
> Under the nettles they are gathered together.
> Fools, even those without a name,
> They were scourged from the land (Job 30:5-8).

In this passage one sees the progression of isolation. First, there is alienation. "They are driven from the community..." They have no meaningful relationships. They have not expe-rienced brotherhood or union with others in the society. Such alienation goes deeper if there has been no bonding in the home. The community expresses rejection. "You don't belong here!" "You can't be one of us!" "Go away!" "We don't want you!" Rejection drives them into isolation. Walls go up, communication ceases; emotional isolation comes in.

The next step is separation: "...they dwell in dreadful valleys..." They now have chosen to live apart from the community, without brotherhood, without union. Now they have become wanderers living without any life-support structures of society. They have rejected family, church, and all governing institu-tions; they have chosen to live in isolation. Without the protection of family, church, and community, they are vulner-able to all the hostile forces of evil. They began to live in the holes of the ground and in the rocks. Desolation and isolation describe the life of the wanderer. He is determined to be free, without authority, without limitations, without responsibility. He separates himself from the community. He has become a wanderer without destiny. He lives only for the moment.

Third, there is the expression of pain as they cry out among the bushes. Separated from the community, rejecting all life support structures, they now experience the pain of isolation. Who can measure the pain of a human soul that cries out for love, for meaning, for comfort? "Cry out" could also be translated "bray"; as the wild ass brays in the wilderness, so they lift their voice. Nothing expresses desolation and hopelessness more than music that fills the air with cries of futility. A song in the 1960's by Paul Simon expresses the pain and isolation of that generation:

> *I am a rock, I am an island.*
> *And a rock feels no pain;*
> *And an island never cries.*

Fourth, in their isolation wanderers seek union: they gather together under the nettles. Pain can become a bonding agent. Yet there is little comfort, only the nettles to gather around. The nettle is a small bush that stings and irritates the skin upon contact. There is no comfort in this community. Life in this community has become a bare existence without meaning. Each day wanderers face emptiness.

Fifth, there is the alienation of fathers' hearts. "Fools, even those without a name" speaks of a generation that has not known their fathers. Totally contrary to nature, fathers' hearts have turned away from their children. In a future chapter we will discuss the reason for this circumstance, but the fact is that most of the deeper problems coming out of childhood come from the alienation of fathers' hearts. Not experiencing the bonding of a father's love drives them into isolation.

Note the state of the human soul; it has become a desert. There is nothing to sustain life, only rocks, bushes, nettles, and holes in the ground. The wanderer dwells in this place, separated from God, from man, and from himself. He lives in isolation.

Addictive Behavior

Isolation is the number-one problem in this society. The breakdown of the family and the lack of brotherhood in the community has left a generation living in a vacuum of emotional needs. Without union, without bonding, they live in emptiness and spaciousness. Without purpose and meaning in life, they live for the moment, hoping to experience something that will make life worthwhile. Addiction meets the need! It dulls the pain; it becomes the way to escape futility and fear. This generation has lost its way; it has been born in an addictive culture.

What roots of this culture produce addictive behavior? What within man causes him to adopt behavior contrary to life? To come to the point quickly, the basic premise is that the roots of addiction come out of alienation. Isolation produces addictive behavior. We will now take an inside look at the wanderer.

First, the wanderer is without union. Here one discovers a basic need of the addict. The lack of brotherhood and community have left him empty and alone. A sense of spaciousness fills his life. He lives in a vacuum. There is not a sense of belonging. There are no meaningful relationships; he lives under a spirit of rejection. Along with this vacuum is much fear. The fear of abandonment is the strongest fear he faces, but there are the fears of rejection and of failure. These fears rule over his mind and emotions, holding him captive. Through addiction he seeks to escape his fears. There is the deep need to enter into union with another person, to be in harmony with the universe, to experience a sense of belonging. The addiction becomes the way of breaking isolation.

Second, the wanderer is alienated from himself. Living under rejection he comes to reject himself. Self-hatred and self-rejection are deep expressions of alienation within. There follows a growing isolation from people. He becomes self-centered and develops a narcissistic personality. Everything evolves around his needs, his problems, his pleasure, et cetera. In relationships he is manipulating and clinging. Looking for one person that will bring meaning and worth to his life, he draws his life from that person. He is introverted, indulgent, entertainment-oriented, living vicariously through the experiences of others, caught up in delusions of himself. Lust and perversion tend to rule over his thoughts. In his isolation he loses perspective, and he has difficulty facing reality.

Within this isolation is the need for transcendence. He reaches for what is beyond the bounds of human cognition and thought. The emptiness and loneliness in which he lives drive him to find meaning in life. The addiction lifts him out of reality, releases him from spaciousness, and helps him to live momentarily in a warm and meaningful world. Fears subside, and he is able to see himself in a completely different way. He finds hope for himself as a person.

Third, the wanderer lives in futility. Here is one of the basic causes of addictive behavior. He is failure-oriented, without purpose, and with no sense of destiny. A sense of futility prevails over his every attempt to succeed; each effort is doomed to fail. A sense of pessimism sees the existing world in the worst possible way: evil in life outweighs the good; nothing will turn out right. He struggles with hopelessness and despair. He comes to the existential view that man exists in a purposeless universe opposed by a hostile environment. Sinking down in a state of passivity, he is unable to make decisions and follow through any plan that would change his situation. Double-minded, without strength of endurance, he is easily discouraged. Not willing to go through the pain of failure, not accepting the discipline necessary to succeed, he easily gives up. This attitude is futility.

He has great need to be invincible. His addiction allows him to experience invincibility. In his addiction he feels, "I can do anything!" "No one can stop me!" "I am in control!" He feels what he has never experienced before. Suddenly he is somebody; he can do something worthwhile; he can succeed in life. He is now free from failure.

Out of futility comes the need for immortality. If life seems meaningless, there is the need for something to make it meaningful. Man waits for destiny, seeks for continuity, and shouts, "I am here!" The big question within him is, Does anyone know I am here? Other questions also come, Is this all there is? and Can I do anything that will make my life worthwhile? When one's life seems futile, the negative answers will drive him to escape the painful searching. Again a certain pessimism will drive him. Perhaps through his addiction he can touch eternity and achieve immortality. Perhaps he can discover meaning in life, or will he just give up completely?

Fourth, the wanderer is full of pain. Bruised and hurting he struggles through life as a wounded person. At times anger and hostility express his inward pain. At other times withdrawn, fearful, distrusting, and hiding, he covers the hurt inside. Pulled between opposite emotions, unpredictable in behavior, he becomes fragmented and broken without self-control. The pain can be so intense he will do anything to escape. The addiction becomes the way to find some release. The need to suspend time allows him to escape reality and pain, enter another dimension, and get control. Who can measure the pain of the human soul? Can there be release and healing?

Fifth, the wanderer is full of shame and guilt. Hiding and covering oneself are also very much parts of addictive behavior. Not willing to admit to himself nor to others that he is out of control, he covers his addiction and hides his actions; he will not admit there is a problem. He holds on to the image that he is in control of his life. Perhaps he does not want to disappoint and cause others pain, so he continues to hide. Yet inside, the guilt and shame cause him to go deeper into the addiction. Somehow he must forget he is caught and held captive by something he has used to gain control of his life. All the needs of the addict come into the picture: the need to suspend time, the need to be invincible, the need to be transcendent and immortal, and the need to find perfect union.

Chapter Six

The Performer

A contemporary of the Australian aboriginal is the Asian people of Japan. For thousands of years this people lived in isolation. Only in the past century did they open their ports for trade, and this change came about by force rather than choice. This isolated nation transformed itself into an industrialized power in just half a century. By the 1930s the Japanese began a venture of world conquest. They extended their borders into China, Korea, Malaysia, Singapore, Indonesia, and the islands of the Pacific. This conquest ended in 1945, with their defeat in World War II. The bombing of allied planes caused severe damage to every major city of this island nation. At the end of the war all their industries were shattered; their economy was destroyed. They had lost everything.

Within twenty years the Japanese completely rebuilt their country into the greatest industrial nation in the world, and became a top competitor for the world market. Japan is now the leading ship-builder and producer of iron and steel, motor vehicles, precision tools and electronic equipment. It is justly famous for cameras and lenses. It has a booming chemical industry and produces textiles and manufactures paper. All this production has come about with almost no natural resources. How could this industrialization have happen? The nation utilized the only natural resource they had, their people. They converted their people into an industrial machine whose production has exceded every industrial nation in the world today. This is an amazing story of a people who lived most of their history in isolation. Only in 1970, did the Emperor Hirohito make a visit outside his country, the first ever by a reigning sovereign.

Now we behold an interesting phenomenon: out of isolation can come intense activity and development. This transformation is true for not only a nation, but also the individual as well. In the biblical account one finds this phenomenon. Cain in his isolation became a builder. Intense activity and the building of a society provided man with purpose and affluence. Cain determined to overcome the curse of isolation and purposelessness. The Scripture says, "Then Cain went out from the presence of the Lord, and settled in the land of Nod... And Cain had relations with his wife and she conceived, and gave birth to Enoch; and he built a city, and called the name of the city Enoch, after the name of his son" (Genesis 4:16,17). From his descendents came artists, agriculturists, and industrialists. These people were skilled in their trades and inventors of implements of bronze and iron. In this time of intense development an affluent society came forth. Man was no longer a wanderer; man now lived in a city. Does the city take away man's isolation?

A culture filled with isolation will give priority to performance and success. Man will begin a search for significance. Isolation has left an underlying sense of worthlessness and purposelessness. Man will go one of two ways: either he will live under rejection and see only failure in his life, or he will not admit to failure of any kind and live under perfectionism. One is failure-oriented, while the other is performance-oriented. One sinks down into purposelessness; the other finds purpose through what he can achieve. One accepts worthlessness and gives up, but the other determines to excel and create worth through what he can do. Both live in a vacuum; both are driven; both develop addictive behavior. Isolation will either drive one into hopeless wandering or else drive one to find worth and purpose through success. The underlying problem is a sense of emptiness coming from a vacuum within. Some have called it "the hole in the soul." Isolation creates this vacuum.

In isolation one sees two extremes. The author knew a family that had two sons: one was a wanderer; the other, a performer. One lived on the streets and wandered from place to place. He had no destination or purpose in life. His lifestyle had been a wanderer from the time he had dropped out of high school. He was willing to risk everything just for a moment of the surreal. For him wandering meant freedom. He died on the street, stabbed by another addict. The other son excelled in school and became a banker. He wore fine clothes and drove nice cars. He was successful. Yet he never married; he has lived alone. This brother is just as isolated as the other; they both lived in a vacuum. Men make a choice which way they will go. Some choose to live under failure and remain wanderers the rest of their lives, while others that are able fill their isolation with achievement and performance. Inside is an emptiness that drives both the wanderer and the performer.

The Kingdom of Self

Man may choose to fill his emptiness with activity. With a determination to overcome isolation, with a decision to find purpose in life, man sets the course of his life to realize his search for significance. He cannot accept failure as the way of life; the life of the wanderer lived in meaninglessness is not acceptable to him. He will build, he will make something of himself. Success means self-worth, significance, and purpose in life. Whatever it takes he will put out the effort to reach his goals. So he enters into a mode of performance that will produce for him all the things he desires. What comes forth is the kingdom of self.

Isolation in society creates a selfish society. Man becomes occupied with his security, comfort, rights, welfare and happiness. Privacy becomes a main concern in his life. He will pull out of the system as much as possible, and then withdraw to hide and keep for himself what he has taken. This behavior is called "hoarding and hiding." It is characteristic of the man that lives for himself. His idol is the system that gives him what he wants. (Jesus calls it the god of Mammon, Matthew 6:24). Riches and wealth are foremost in his thought and effort. He builds high walls around himself that give him security and privacy. The truth is, he has become more and more isolated as a person. He is trapped inside the walls he himself has built. He has filled the vacuum within with materialism and power.

A certain pride comes to the man that isolates him further. He has built an image for himself from his performance. Success has created an image of worth. He dedicates his whole life to creating and maintaining this image. This image of self, created out of performance, is filled with pride. The Scripture speaks of men who "...have set up their idols in their hearts..." (Ezekiel 14:3). They will sacrifice everything to maintain this image, including family. Basically the man is a perfectionist whose self-image and self-worth depend upon his performance. Perfectionism never gives him rest; restlessness drives him; nothing is ever enough. The emptiness inside drives him to build bigger and better things. The image of pride is never satisfied; it continually cries, "More! More! More!"

Within this kingdom is very little life. He gives his life and energy to an image. Isolated as a person, he is impersonal in relationships, preferring groups rather than one-on-one. Superficial and remote, no one really knows him. He is the performer that knows how to please people and fulfill his role. In the work place he can be intimidating, demanding, and angry. Others see him as brash, hard, and insensitive in getting what he wants. He is goal-oriented rather than people-oriented. He becomes a machine that drives himself and others to perform. No life comes out of a machine.

At home there is a certain severity of attitude toward his family. His busy schedule does not allow him to spend time with his family. The isolation within does not release him to build strong personal relationships with his children. His approach is a performance-based relationship; if they do well, he accepts them; if they do badly, he rejects them. Generally he is communicates rejection through his performance-oriented base. The following characterize his relationship with his children: little time spent, inability to express love, toleration of their presence, punishment to vent hostility, open statements of rejection, verbal acceptance with emotional rejection, making all the decisions for them or else too little guidance, inability to release the children to be people, rejection of children because he sees himself in them, holding other things or persons more important than family, critical and perfectionistic attitudes. The bottom line is, he cannot express love and acceptance; he does not have a father's heart.

In response to this attitude of severity, certain attitudes develop within the children that say, "You reject me; I will reject you! You hurt me; I will hurt you!" The alienation grows until there is complete isolation. The following reflect these attitudes: resentment and bitterness, loss of communication, rebellion against authority, ambivalence, and distrust. The bottom line is, since there has been no bonding with his children, alienation separates the children from their father.

Perhaps it is good to mention the wife — what goes on with her? Basically he will love his wife as he loves himself; therefore, he will be demanding a level of performance that fits his expectations. She must fit the image and role of the model woman, whatever he perceives that to be. The wife lives in a vacuum of unmet needs. She feels unloved, empty, lonely, and resentful. It is difficult for her to relate to a husband that is generally cold and insensitive; consequently, she withdraws into her own private area of isolation. Idiosyncracies and compulsions will become a problem in her life, and then addictions will develop.

Addictive Behavior

The performer's drive to excel will carry him right into addictive behavior. First and foremost, the performer must be in control. Sustained pressure upon him will cause him to reach for substances to relieve the pressure and put him on top. The same needs as the wanderer drive him. He has need to suspend time; that is, he must put as much as possible into every hour. He lives with a full schedule that demands his time and energy. Stuff as much as possible into the schedule; accelerate the motor; turn on the juices. Produce! Produce! Produce! He maintains a continued high with the pressure for performance.

He must maintain a sense of being invincible. He presents the image of the superman; nothing is too difficult; he always has the answers. So he puts himself into every problem, feeling that the life of the whole organization rests upon him. The performance must go on; he becomes the great savior; every-one looks to him. Through this performance he is filling the emptiness inside with pride. He is invincible, he is in control.

All the effort is worthwhile if he can become immortal. He will make sure that no one forgets him. He will leave behind his monuments of success. He will fill his house with reminders of his superior ability. He will do everything possible to become irreplaceable. Everyone shall remember the person of great worth, because his performance surpassed all others. He was the best!

Yet, there is another side to this person. That which was foremost in his life, to be in control, is also absent in his life. Caught in hidden vices, lusts, and addictions, he drives himself into isolation. He finds himself being compulsive in matters of money, time management, health, recreation, community service, and privacy. Money becomes the source of power that gives him control and personal worth. Eating can be compulsive along with alcohol consumption. In areas in which the person is not in control, he becomes compulsive and driven. Traits of addictive behavior soon appear in his life.

Man cannot become a machine without compulsions and addictions resulting. Returning to the example of the Japanese nation that converted its people into an industrial machine, the high performance rate required in the work place put tremendous pressure upon the people. Unable to accept failure, they allow the workplace to drive them to excel. Their personal worth depends upon their performance. To fail is to experience disgrace that degrades that person of all personal worth. Consequently, they give long, arduous hours on the job. The average Japanese works six days a week; many arrive home after the children are in bed. With only one day to spend with family, they dedicate their lives to performance on the job. To fill this personal void, they nurture themselves with material possessions and long-planned-for vacations. Foremost is their sustained performance and continual production — that goes on and on. As a result, the highest per capita alcohol consumption is in Japan. Hour after hour the Japanese occupy gambling houses filled with machines trying to fill the void in their lives.

The Machine

A basic question every man asks himself is, "Can I produce enough to be successful?" In a society where isolation is prevalent, people will give their attention to success and performance. Success becomes the purpose for life. In the process man becomes a machine whose sole purpose becomes production. To be diligent and hard-working is one thing, but to be driven as a machine into an existence whose sole purpose is to produce, that is another thing. Here modern man struggles. How can he be productive and successful without becoming a machine?

First, consider the purpose and end of a machine. Its purpose is production. Without production it is worthless. Its goal is to reach the full potential, produce as much as possible, last as long as possible, and then go into discard when it wears out. The value of the performer's life depends upon his performance, so when he can no longer perform, he loses all value. The society that puts all value upon success and performance drives its people into a mechanical existence. What happens to machines when they can no longer perform? People get rid of them, as they are worthless.

What really gives purpose and value to life? The purpose of life is to give life. A machine cannot do this. Life comes out of life; it cannot be manufactured. Rather than placing the value of a life on performance, we should measured life by what it gives to others. Where the performer lives his life in isolation and selfishness, the life-giver lays his life down for others. His life is given. This truth brings one to the heart of Christianity. "God so loved...that He gave His only begotten Son..." (John

3:16). Only love can produce life in another, only love will lay down its life for another; only love will give everything; only love finds value in everyone. Here is purpose, here is value, that "...you love one another" (John 13:34). Jesus brings the final word on purpose and worth, "He who keeps his life for himself shall lose it, but he who gives his life shall find it" (Matthew 10:39 Paraphrased). The kingdom of self must come down; we must abolish isolation; only then will life come forth. God has called us to be life-givers, not machines.

Chapter Seven

Lawlessness

The Twentieth Century brought into the world unprecedented development, which was as a seed that lay dormant in the ground, and suddenly, it burst forth with such force that it totally transformed the world of man. Within one century technology took man from steam engines to nuclear power, from the first wireless message to space satelites, from silent movies to videos, from radios to television, from knowledge stored in books to computer chips that stored complete libraries, from the first flight at Kitty Hawk to jet airliners that brought the whole world within a one-day trip, from bare household necessities to a multiple assortment of appliances that made everything easy, and from isolation to a world market that brought wealth and goods from all over the world. Science seemed to have found the answer to all of man's problems. Everything seemed to agree with Charles Darwin's theory of progressive evolution; man had joined with nature to discover an evolution of development that would bring him into a utopia of dignity, freedom, and security. Man was now able to free himself from disease, poverty, and prejudice; or so he thought.

The utopia that science and politics built was not all good. Regression into the massive savagery of two world wars accompanied the unleashing of unparalleled progress. Violence filled the earth as powerful weapons of destruction destroyed nations. During the latter part of the century there was a major breakdown of values in society. A fragmentation of the family and the decline of the basic support structures of society brought forth an alienated generation. A sexual revolution released sexual promiscuity in society that revived veneral diseases people thought had been irradicated. The spread of the dread HIV virus caused the death of tens of thousands. An alarming boom in prostitution debased thousands of women and children whom their owners held captive in some nations of the world. Corruption entered society through crime, pornography, gambling, drugs, and prostitution. Society lost its soul, it lost its way. General moral decline came at a time of massive development. This decline is the enigma of this age. Man has not learned to govern himself because he is still living in lawlessness as an individual. Here in lawlessness one finds the last expression of alienation preceding judgment. Ultimately, alienation will reject authority, refuse restraint, and give itself to lawlessness.

One other society compares to this age in its development and decay, that of Cain. Within eight generations that society destroyed itself. Violence and corruption accompanied its intense development. Everyone lived for himself. There was no government to restrain man. He was free to do whatever was good in his own eyes. The foundations were laid in humanism that proclaimed happiness for all humanity. The humanists preached the good life through self-actualization, self-determination, and self-indulgence. They emphasized feelings rather than moral responsibility. They declared nothing was really wrong or bad of itself; morality depended upon the consequences of an act rather than absolutes of righteousness. Without being bound by absolutes of right and wrong, man was free to live life for its own sake. An existential philosophy ruled the day: If it feels good, it must be good. Jesus described that society, "They were eating, they were drinking, they were marrying, they were being given in marriage, until the day that Noah entered the ark, and the flood came and destroyed them all" (Luke 17:27). Obsessed with the "good life," they were unaware of coming judgment. The lawlessness of the day totally corrupted them.

Violence characterized the society of Cain. When the sons of God took wives of the daughters of men breaking the order of righteousness, something was birthed that had severe consequences for that society. (Read Genesis 6:1-12.) From this mixture the Nephilim were born who were wicked men. "Then the Lord saw that the wickedness of man was great on the earth, and that every intent of the thoughts of his heart was only evil continually" (verses 4,5). The giants in Scripture were always synonymous with evil and always in opposition to the righteous. We could compare the giants to the role models of society today found in entertainment, that influence a younger generation to lawlessness and unrighteousness. As lawlessness broke down the order of righteousness within that culture, the foundations of society were destroyed. Judgment followed.

The Alienation of Fathers' Hearts

A phenomenon of the Twentieth Century is the alienation of fathers' hearts from their children. At no other time in history do we find that one's culture has destroyed the union between father and children. In previous chapters we made observations about the wanderer and the performer, that help to explain this phenomenon. In a time of intense development family relationships tend to break down. The drive to find the "good life" becomes first in man's priorities. People lay everything upon the altar of success and materialism. The Scriptures speak of a time before the end when fathers' hearts would be turned away from children, children's hearts would be turned away from fathers, and a curse would come into society. This alienation is a sign of the last days.

"Behold, I am going to send you Elijah the prophet before the coming of the great and terrible day of the Lord. And he will restore the hearts of the fathers to their children, and the hearts of the children to their fathers, lest I come and smite the land with a curse" (Malachi 4:5,6). Alienation brings a curse in the land. Lawlessness and rebellion come out of hearts alienated from their fathers. Alienation begins with the fathers. When fathers' hearts are alienated from their children, children's hearts will be alienated from fathers, and then the curse comes into the land. Alienation causes children to go down a road of destruction: from resentment to bitterness, from bitterness to rebellion, from rebellion to lawlessness and witchcraft. When children's hearts are turned away from fathers, they become the wanderers lost in society with no sense of value, no purpose nor discernment of evil; full of sin, rebellion, rejection and self-hatred; insecure and immature; ungrateful; self-centered. Job described that generation as "Fools, even those without a name" (Job 30:8).

The curse comes through violence and insanity. Alienation has released violence in society. Crime has filled the prisons, and the mentally disturbed have filled the hospitals. Filled with hostility, and driven to violence, their actions and behavior do not come short of insanity. The bizarre, perverted, indulgent, addicted, all make up a generation that has turned within. Isolated within and alienated without, they live in pain, fear, and rejection. With neither bonding nor purpose, a generation lives closed up within a darkness filled with the imagined and the surreal. Alienation has cut them loose from all moorings of family and culture. Hostile without, fearful within, the curse of alienation comes into society. One finds a society out of control.

Hedonism is another part of the curse. Pleasure-seeking becomes a way of life, the principle good, and the motivation for every action. People seek pleasure in every form, and the inventors of pleasure become the heroes. Soon the normal no longer satisfies, and people desire perverted forms of pleasure. Ever searching for the exotic with the familiar, the base with the natural, man's taste for a new experience drives him until he becomes reprobate in his thinking. As it was before the flood when "...all flesh had corrupted their way upon the earth" (Genesis 6:12), corruption now fills society.

Children formed under alienation become isolated, rebellious, and violent. The father's absence creates a vacuum that isolates the children. Even though they may be housed, clothed, and entertained, the emptiness inside leaves them lonely and unfulfilled. Life loses its meaning.

The Nature of Rebellion

Whatever may be the behavior in society, rebellion within the human soul alienates man from God and man from man. One sees the nature or working of rebellion within in three ways: it refuses to bend its will, it refuses to give its heart, and it refuses to release control.

Good mental health is dependent upon the person's being able to submit his will. One psychiatrist with many years of experience noted that every person he had known with good mental health had submitted his will to something or someone higher than himself. The truth is, an unsubmitted will finds no peace. Wilful people are "...like the tossing sea, for it cannot be quiet, and its waters toss up refuse and mud. `There is no peace,' says my God, `for the wicked'" (Isaiah 57:20,21). Constantly agitated, driven by inner compulsions, unable to be still, their lives consist of incessant striving. The person who cannot bend his will finds no rest.

Rebellion does not give its heart; it refuses to bond with another. A woman who has never been bonded to her father will find it difficult to bond with any man. For some the reason may be hurts and pain, and for others it may be pride and independence; the fact is, alienation isolates the heart. This emotional isolation in many cases creates a Jezebel spirit that wants the attention of all and commits to no one. This problem is not in women only, but men likewise are alienated in heart. In alienation lust becomes the master and robs a man of a father's heart.

The Spirit of the Lord cries out concerning those who cannot give their hearts, "This people honors Me with their lips, but their heart is far away from Me. But in vain do they worship Me, teaching as their doctrines the precepts of men" (Matthew 15:8,9).

We see in this scripture one with an independent spirit that performs well, yet misses the essential quality of worship which is union with God. In faith as well, he does not have that quality of dependence that brings forth the will of God. His relationship to God is built upon performance and within his heart there is not union with Him.

Alienation creates that independent spirit that has to be in control. Control becomes the issue for them who have never bent their wills nor given their hearts. At any cost they will hold on and resist. It is almost impossible for them to think of releasing control of their lives. Strong wills and isolated hearts maintain control. They force their way through life, unsubmitted and uncommitted. Demanding and angry, they determine to achieve their goals. A strong, independent spirit prevails. Unbending and not bonding to anyone, they live in alienation. Rebellion refuses to release control.

A Way of Life

Lawlessness is sin coming out of rebellion. As lawlessness prevails in society, rebellion prevails within man. The consequence of sin is slavery rather than freedom. Lust and perversion rule over man. All kinds of compulsions indicate a person out of control. The way of life of the rebellious refuses restraint, resists authority, and indulges the flesh. Many addictions enslave man as he makes his declaration of independence. The bottom line is this: when one rejects authority, the body rules over man. A person who has never allowed authority to operate in his life will experience enslavement to lust. The body is a cruel master. One's soul will hear its demands and its cravings will not go away. Man controlled by his lust must deal with lawlessness because of rebellion.

One young man was struggling to overcome lust. He had experienced freedom from homosexuality through his commitment to Christ. In his struggle with lust he constantly found himself defeated as he gave over to masturbation. Try as he may, there seemed to be no victory over the lust that drove him to this practice. One day the counselor asked him if he had ever submitted to his father's authority. He remembered that even though he had obeyed outwardly the commands of his father, the lack of union with his father had caused him to resent and reject his father's authority. That lack of union not only led him into homosexuality, but also established rebellion as a way of life. There could be no victory over lust until he confessed and repented of rebellion against authority.

Disorder and procrastination come out of rebellion. When one rejects discipline, one creates a way of life that leaves him disoriented and purposeless. Many unfinished tasks remain from day to day. The further one goes, the more disorder he finds in his life in every area. He has never submitted to the order of righteousness; authority has not had its formation in his life; he has not accepted responsibility; he has rejected the discipline of work. Without strength to endure, he finds the flesh with its indulgent nature ruling over him. Compulsions and addictions tend to fill the void. He has lost the way; things are out of control. Passivity comes in upon him.

Rebellion stops the learning process. We hear much about our educational system and its failure to teach the children. Some would say the fault lies with the teacher and teaching methods, while others would attribute the failure to the curriculum. However, one must consider the premise that children who never learn to submit to authority are not teachable. Without authority, the learning process does not take place. There has to be submission to the discipline of learning. Rebellion has a certain effect upon the mind that causes it to resist the discipline of listening and learning.

God spoke to the prophet and said, "Son of man, you live in the midst of the rebellious house, who have eyes to see but do not see, ears to hear but do not hear; for they are a rebellious house" (Ezekiel 12:2). Rebellion has a way of closing the eyes and ears so that a person does not see and hear. Through another prophet God said, "You will keep on hearing, but will not understand; and you will keep on seeing, but will not perceive; for the heart of this people has become dull" (Acts 28:21,27). Rebellion makes the heart dull, the ears heavy, and the eyes dim so that there is no understanding. The learning process stops.

Rebellion is an open door to witchcraft. "For rebellion is as the sin of divination, and insubordination is as iniquity and idolatry..." (I Samuel 15:23). A person with an unsubmitted will seeks to establish control through spiritual means. Through witchcraft man becomes his own god. The powers of darkness come to serve his purposes. Having rejected the knowledge of God, man desires to see the unseen, know the unknown, and experience the supernatural. Witchcraft submits to no authority; it is the ultimate exercise of man's will in rebellion. The result of witchcraft is darkness and ignorance over the minds of the people. The Scriptures speak of "...the covering which is over all peoples, even the veil which is stretched over all nations" (Isaiah 25:7). The darkness of witchcraft covers the mind so that a person loses the knowledge of God. Once the powers of darkness begin to operate within the mind, man experiences deception that brings him under the curse.

Chapter Eight

A Righteous Man

In 1970, the author experienced a visitation of the Lord that transformed his life and ministry. Having served as a missionary in Brazil for the previous nine years, he was in a state of burn-out both physically and spiritually. This visitation was the author's salvation, and he waited for wonderful things to come forth in his life- perhaps a world-wide ministry. To the author's surprise and chagrin, the Lord spoke to him that he should learn to be a father. In his disappointment he questioned the Lord about this turn of events. He was already the father of three and waiting for the birth of another; he provided and cared for his family; what more could the Lord expect of him?

The Lord continued to speak, "Have you considered Noah?" No, the author had not considered Noah to be a model for ministry. Certainly, Noah was a good boat builder, but what missionary would want to preach 120 years without a convert? The inner voice continued, "How many sons did he have?" Three sons, of course, but what significance did this fact have to fatherhood? "How many sons did he take into the ark with him?" All of them, he answered. "In what kind of day did Noah live?" The author knew it was the worst time of all history for a righteous man to rear a family. Then a question came with penetrating force, "How did Noah bring every son into the ark when every other father and son were living in rebellion and lawlessness?" He did not know the answer to that question: God now had his total attention. The truth of the matter came to him that he would possibly be living in times similiar to Noah, so how could he bring every son into the ark of the Lord without losing one? This matter was very important.

What do the Scriptures say? "...Noah was a righteous man, blameless in his time; Noah walked with God. And Noah became the father of three sons: Shem, Ham, and Japheth. Now the earth was corrupt in the sight of God, and the earth was filled with violence. And God looked on the earth, and behold, it was corrupt; for all flesh had corrupted their way upon the earth" (Genesis 6:9-12). Noah received instructions from the Lord to build an ark for the salvation of his household, because judgment was coming in a flood that would destroy mankind and every living thing. What turned the hearts of Noah's sons away from the world of that day? What caused them to become involved with their father in an endeavor that caused ridicule and rejection? What kind of father was Noah?

A Father's Heart

Noah was a father with a father's heart. No alienation separated him from his sons. They had his heart and he had their hearts. They stood together in a critical time; they were united because their hearts were bonded. This bonding is the first key in bringing sons into the ark. When fathers have the hearts of their children, the children will follow them into the ark. In this statement is rest and confidence: a father's love will prevail. In an evil day children will look to fathers first to show them the way. When children look at fathers as all-knowing, the greatest in the world, the bonding must take place; otherwise, the opportunity passes and a second chance comes with delay and difficulty.

For them to be strong to resist the influence of an evil day, children must know who they are and what they are worth. A child who has never had his father's love and acceptance will be weak and his peers will easily lead him. The search for identity and worth will cause him to conform to his culture and friends. Not able to stand alone or be different, he continually will seek for acceptance. He will live in a vacuum that draws rejection from the father relationship. His self-image and self-worth being unformed will make him vulnerable, weak, and fearful. He will not endure the pain of any rejection coming from friends, because it touches his deepest insecurity. He does not know who he is or what he is worth, so he is willing to go along. The girl who has not known a father's love will tend to be promiscuous in order to receive the attention and love of men. Weak, vulnerable children come out of alienation.

Noah's sons were strong men; they knew who they were and what they were worth. They were able to stand against the temptations and pressure of their day. They could stand alone. They drew from the strength of their father; they accepted the convictions of their father; they had the heart of their father. Noah's sons were a reflection of Noah. They knew who they were because they knew their father. Out of fathers' hearts flows the love that forms the children's self-image and self-worth. This love is the most valuable gift a father passes on to his sons and daughters. We must emphasize that both sons and daughters receive the formation of themselves as persons from relationship with their fathers. The father's heart forms the child.

The second key in bringing sons and daughters into the ark is a father's authority. Fathers will lead children who submit themselves to them. The bent will goes hand-in-hand with the bonded heart. Even as the father's heart forms the person of the child, the father's authority forms his character. Person and character, both essential, make a total man or woman. A balance between love and authority brings perfect formation. In the absence of love, authority can be harsh, cruel, and unjustly severe. In the absence of authority, love can be indulgent and tolerant to excess. Fathers need to be lovingly firm and firmly loving so that godly authority forms their children.

An essential function of authority is the formation of character. Through the imposition of discipline character is formed. Discipline is a process of training that develops self-control, endurance, and good behavior. One can see the principle of authority in the exercise of chastisement and correction, instruction and training, responsibility and accountability. Without obedience the process does not take place. Without the exercise of authority, there is no formation of character. Character is formed like clay in the hand of the potter, who takes the clay and forms it into a particular design. This concept is totally opposite to the modern-day philosophy of leaving a child untouched and unformed. This society tends to substitute intelligence for virtue, beauty for character, and materialism for worth. These three highest social values of the day do not necessarily require character. If one can know enough, be becoming enough, and own enough, people look upon him as successful. Yet what he is as a person can be immeasurably short of one who is honest, loyal, faithful, courageous, humble, grateful, diligent, and dependable. In these traits character is found.

A Father's Authority

Noah was a man of authority. Blameless and righteous before the Lord, he stood without fear before men. He was not legalistic, perfectionistic, controlling, or angry. He walked in love with godly authority and worked righteousness. He could stand with authority because he was submitted to God. The same relationship he had with God the Father he established with his sons. The world respected him for his righteousness; his sons honored him for his godliness. He was strong, he was gentle. Submitted to God, he walked in obedience. God commanded, he obeyed. He listened to God's voice, so his sons listened to his voice. They honored him because he honored God. They obeyed him because he obeyed God. The formation of righteousness took place in his sons because he established godly authority in his home.

A father should be "...like a refuge from the wind, and a shelter from the storm, like streams of water in a dry country, like the shade of a huge rock in a parched land" (Isaiah 32:2). These scenes from nature describe a man with authority. The first purpose of a man with authority is to protect. He shall be a refuge and a shelter; those under him shall find safety. Because much evil is in the world, the man in authority stands to face the wind and the storm. Authority is given to protect those under it.

Like "...streams of water in a dry country," authority gives life. Whether in the home or church those in authority should be like a stream flowing through dry country, bringing life to all they touch. Such life is a most essential quality of authority. If it is not life-giving, then authority has degenerated into a spirit of control, whose chief goal is to maintain control over others. With control comes manipulation, intimidation, exaltation, and isolation. Whereas authority works through love, the spirit of control works through rejection. Generally control is performance-based in its acceptance, perfectionistic in its demands, and legalistic in its stand. Very seldom pleased, it drives rather than guides; it dwells upon the negative rather than developing the positive; it cuts down rather than builds up; it does not give itself to disciple; it does not nurture; there is no bonding; it does not have a father's heart. This perversion of authority has entered the home and church, quenching the Spirit and bringing death. "Now...where the Spirit of the Lord is, there is liberty" (II Corinthians 3:17), and where there is liberty there is life. Each man in authority should be a "life-giving spirit" (I Corinthians 15:45).

Like "...the shade of a huge rock in a parched land," authority gives rest. The character of the righteous man is to live in peace. "The work of righteousness will be peace, and the service of righteousness, quietness and confidence forever. Then my people will live in a peaceful habitation, and in secure dwellings and in undisturbed resting places" (Isaiah 32:17,18). When godly authority has established the order of righteousness, peace will come into the home. Without the exercise of authority, confusion, disorder, and strife fill the house. Rest comes to those who come under authority. A righteous man shall be as a large rock, giving rest to those who abide under him.

A righteous man teaches and instructs those under his author-ity. This impartation of truth and wisdom opens the eyes of the blind and the ears of the deaf. "Then the eyes of those who see will not be blinded, and the ears of those who hear will listen. And the mind of the hasty will discern the truth, and the tongue of the stammerers will hasten to speak clearly" (Isaiah 32:3,4). Here one discovers the marvelous power of truth. Until one learns truth the eyes and ears remained closed, the mind runs unbridled over the earth, and foolishness comes out of the mouth. Because of the lack of instruction in righteousness, "a fool speaks nonsense, and his heart inclines toward wicked-ness, to practice ungodliness and to speak error against the Lord..." (vs. 6). One without instruction becomes a rogue whose "...weapons are evil; he devises wicked schemes to destroy the afflicted with slander..." (vs.7). When fools and rogues rise to places of authority, the people suffer, "but the noble man devises noble plans; and by noble plans he stands" (vs.8). Such is the character of the righteous. Righteous men bring forth righteous sons who will establish righteousness in the land.

Chapter Nine

God the Father

A strange thing has happened in the latter part of the Twentieth Century: women have rejected the Father image of God. A strong surge of feminism has attempted to revive the spirit of the ancient goddesses. Feminism declares that patriarchy is responsible for all death-dealing technology. It further declares that ours is an artificial culture predicated upon silencing of women's experience, upon soul-deadening education, the substitute of power for love in marriages and families, and upon all the woman-hating atrocities of history. Feminists are attempting to shatter the language and ideology of a patriarchal society and project the primal power of women's spirit and female consciousness. Their final goal is the reclamation of female energy and the revival of these ancient goddesses. They present a woman-centered cosmology based on the principle of the divine Feminine imminent, in woman and nature. Feminists identify the Judeo-Christian tradition as the primary agent of suppression and desecration of the divine spark of female being. Feminists hold that the Judeo-Christian system legitimized absolute male power and replaced the matriarchal cult of the Great Goddess. They have proclaimed war upon patriarchy and have determined to change the image of God as Father.

The struggle with the Father image of God centers around

authority. For some, to envision God as sitting on a throne brings a response of consternation at His being tyrannical, arbitrary, and despotic. For them authority is contrary to the exercise of free will, subjecting them to absolutes of another world. They prefer to be free to exercise their will through a process of reasoning rather than to submit to predetermined laws of righteousness. In the matter of authority, the philosophies of relativism and humanism allow man the freedom he prefers. Man desires to make his own rules rather than to bow down to God. As one can see, the spirit of the age is contrary to an image of God who sits on a throne. The throne which symbolizes His authority and power becomes an obstacle to the natural man who has not yet bowed down. How about the reader? Does the image of God's sitting upon a throne bother you? Who is this Entity that incorporates authority and power within His Person? Perhaps you have struggled with these questions as you have tried to deal with your own experiences with authority.

The order of righteousness rests upon the authority and rule of God. Whether it is the order of life in the universe or the order of righteousness in society, order comes forth out of His authority that His throne symbolizes. To the extent of His authority, righteousness goes forth, and by His authority, righteousness is established. Why does God sit upon a throne? God sits upon a throne to establish the order of His righteousness. "Righteousness and justice are the foundation of Thy throne..." (Psalm 89:14). Righteousness comes out of His authority, authority comes out of His righteousness. One cannot separate the two. God sits on a throne because He is righteous! God will do right, for righteousness is His character. Because of His righteousness, man can trust Him.

Lovingkindness accompanies His authority. We find these two qualities of His fatherhood together. "Righteousness and justice are the foundation of Thy throne; lovingkindness and truth go before Thee" (Psalm 89:14). Kindness is as much His nature as righteousness is His character. Lovingkindness speaks of one who cares, listens, helps, gives of himself, has compassion and is touched by the suffering of others. Lovingkindness is a disposition that extends itself to others without limits; whatever the cost, for whatever time it takes, it will meet the need. Lovingkindness incorporates the full meaning of words such as grace, mercy, loyalty, and love. Approachable and available, in meekness and gentleness, it maintains its presence in faithfulness. Lovingkindness reveals the Father heart of God. He fulfills this Scripture: "Lovingkindness and truth have met together; righteousness and peace have kissed each other" (Psalm 85:10). Lovingkindness comes forth from His throne upon those who conform to His righteousness. God is good!

Having seen the heart of the Father, can anyone refuse to accept Him? "But now, O Lord, Thou art our Father, we are the clay, and Thou our potter; and all of us are the work of Thy hand" (Isaiah 64:8). The formation of God's children comes from the Father's heart and the Father's authority. The balance and work of both conform one to His image and character. The Father sits on the throne. The work of righteousness takes place in a person through submission to the Father. The titles our Father and our Potter reveal the two roles of God in relationship to man. God is Father, God is Potter. A formation of righteousness takes place under His authority as a Father, just like clay in the hand of the potter. The molding and making process are a work of His Fatherhood. Can there be anything less than a response of obedience from those who recognize Him as Father? They become as clay in the hand of the Potter. Having experienced His formation they declare: God is good! God is righteous!

The Spirit of Sonship

"For you have not received a spirit of slavery leading to fear again, but you have received a spirit of adoption as sons by which we cry out, `Abba! Father!'" (Romans 8:15). What is the cry from your heart? Have you ever known a father's love? Have you ever submitted to a father's authority? Perhaps you have only fear and distrust, or maybe resistance and rebellion. Many live under a spirit of slavery because they have never known a father's heart. You can rage, you can fight, you can attempt to destroy the Father image in the heavens, but deep inside woman is the deepest of needs, a desire to be bonded to a father's heart. The alienation of fathers' hearts has brought forth a generation of daughters who refuse to be bonded to God or man.

The image of God as Father is formed by your natural father. What your father was, you project in thought, attitudes, and behavior toward the heavenly Father. Experiences of a negative kind leave lasting impressions that alienate you as a person. If your father was isolated and cold, you will tend to be the same. If your father was too busy to care, so then a certain neglect will also be within you. Perhaps he was just passive and uninvolved in life, a certain don't-care attitude can penetrate you. A parent's perfectionism and rejection can fill a child with much condemnation and self-rejection. If your father was angry and violent, fear and pain can be deep within you. All the pain, neglect, and isolation coming from a father can bring reactions toward God that are very strong. Your feelings toward the heavenly Father generally reflect what is inside you.

A positive image of God as Father is formed by fathers who are faithful, generous, loving, kind, confirming, accepting, attentive, accessible, righteous, and forgiving. Faithfulness says, "I will stand with you; you can depend on me." Generosity says,

"I will meet your needs; you are important to me." Love says, "I accept you; you are mine forever." Attentiveness says, "I care; I am listening to you." Righteousness says, "I will do right; you can trust me." The character and person of the earthly father communicate these messages and create a positive image for the heavenly Father. The immediate response of every child to this father image should be, "Abba! Daddy!"

God the Father wants sons rather than slaves. Those who have never known a father's heart tend to take the slave mentality. In the world during the time of Christ, a Roman household would have two types of persons: the slave and the son. The slave existed to meet the needs of the household. What he could do determined his value. Obedience to commands and rules was the base of his relationship to the head of the household. Then there was the son; he related to the head of the house in a much different way. Compare the two. Whereas the emphasis with the slave was upon what he could do, with the son the emphasis was upon what he could be. The worth of the slave depended upon his serving; the worth of the son came from his birth. The slave's position depended upon a proper response to authority, coming through rules and commands; the son related to authority coming through a father's love. The son had access and freedom in the house; he did not live in fear. In correction there was the tenderness of a father; the father did not expected him to be perfect. The father would be patient as he matured. The father's heart was to give him the best and to prepare him to be heir of his house. The relationship was built upon love rather than law.

What has failed to come forth in the natural can be created in the spiritual. God is calling His children to sonship. "For God has not given us a spirit of timidity, but of power and love and discipline" (II Timothy 1:7). God's sons experience freedom from the fear, timidity, and cowardice of slaves. They know their Father, He is the Head of the house. The heirs of the house shall not fear the slaves. Full of courage, full of faith, they have high expectations and hope for the future. The sons of the house have the provisions of the house; most of all, they have the Father's heart.

For the sons there is power. Men will give responsibility to them, and they will stand erect and face the task without fear. Power comes through sonship. A divine enablement comes with the calling; they are sons of destiny. Ready and able, they will go forth in confidence. "On the day I called Thou didst answer me; Thou didst make me bold with strength in my soul" (Psalm 138:3). Nothing shall be impossible; no mountain shall stand before them. When they cry, "...Grace, grace...", the Father shall respond, "...Not by might nor by power, but by My Spirit..." (Zechariah 4:6,7). In holy alliance with the Father, bonded and free, the sons of the house go forth into the world. The Father will glorify Himself in His sons.

For the sons there is love. Out of a sense of worth they express love without fear. The Father has broken alienation they have suffered; He has bonded them to Himself. No longer isolated and afraid, they now enter into union with other men. Truly they fulfill the prayer of the Son of God, "...[Father, make them] one, just as We are one" (John 17:22). Free from alienation, they bond together as one to become a witness to the whole world that Jesus Christ has come. These become the ministers of reconciliation; they pronounce the glad tidings of salvation. They touch empty and lonely hearts; the wanderers, the performers, the lawless, all respond to the touch of love. Nothing goes deeper, nothing penetrates the deserts of isolation more than love. Filled with His love, the sons of the house go forth into the world.

For the sons there is sound judgment. Confident in making sound decisions, they choose the will of the Father. Without fear of failure, confident in the Father, they bring forth the Kingdom of God on earth. For they "...who know their God will display strength and take action" (Daniel 11:32). Free from passivity, they reach for the will of the Father in heaven and become instruments of that will on earth. Opposition and opposing circumstances do not move them; their minds are fixed, they stand in the discipline of faith. "...Destroying speculations and every lofty thing raised up against the knowledge of God, and...taking every thought captive to the obedience of Christ" (II Corinthians 10:5), they are sons with sound minds. These truly have found freedom; they go forth into the world proclaiming the Kingdom of God has come.

Without Alienation

The heart of the Father is without alienation. "...God was in Christ reconciling the world to Himself..." (II Corinthians 5:19). He loves the sinner! The heart of the Father is clearly revealed in the parable of the prodigal son (Luke 15:11-32). First, the father releases the son giving him his inheritance. Even though the young man leaves the home, the heart of the father goes with him. No one knows how long he waited, but daily he stood by the door looking down the road to see perhaps a familiar figure walking up the road. Many times his heart must have leaped with expectation at the sight of some lone soul coming down the road. Time and time again he was disappointed.

Meanwhile the son was having a good time spending his father's inheritance. He wined and dined, he danced and sang, he entertained many friends, until one day the money was all gone. Now he finds himself alone with friends and money gone.

No one seemed to care that he was hungry. He had no place to sleep; his clothes became dirty and worn. He was nothing more than a begger now. He must have thought about his father many times, but he was too much ashamed to return home. Finally, he found a job tending the swine of a farmer. Hungry, homeless, without a friend in the world, he lived with the pigs. No one would have considered this discarded person worthy of anyone's love, but there was a father who kept waiting. One day this young man made a decision; he would return to his father and ask him to make him one of the hired servants. He was not seeking sonship; he wanted to be only a servant. Even at a long distance the father recognized him — this was his son! He ran to meet him and threw his arms around him. The son was embarrassed; he was dirty, ragged, bearded, smelling like a pig-how could anyone stand to come close to him? The father's heart did not see the dirt nor smell the stench; the father's heart was reaching for the heart of his son. Without hesitation he hugged him; with great joy he received him, not as a slave but as a son. This is the Father heart of God.

Chapter Ten

Like a Bush in the Desert

Bushes grow in the desert. These small growths of vegetation push themselves up through the hot, dry, hard ground. With not enough support from nature to grow tall with trunks and extended branches, they remain small with no trunks, the branches growing out of the roots. Forever bound to the surface of the hot ground, the bush defies nature in order to survive. It is a very humble type of life that gathers no admirers. Scrubby, scratchy, tough, and dry, no one cares to come close. With no practical use to man, the bush continues to live, giving no fruit to eat nor wood with which to build. It dwells in the parched places of the earth, among the rocks, in places uncultivated and uninhabited. Isolated, lonely, barely holding on to life, the bush typifies the person living in alienation. The Scripture describes this person, "For he will be like a bush in the desert and will not see when prosperity comes, but will live in stony wastes in the wilderness, a land of salt without inhabitant" (Jeremiah 17:6).

"For He grew up before Him like a tender shoot, and like a root out of parched ground; He has no stately form or majesty that we should look upon Him, nor appearance that we should be attracted to Him" (Isaiah 53:2). Who is this that comes up out of parched ground? Who is this whose form is not stately or majestic, whose appearance is without beauty to create desire?

81

Is this not the Messiah, the Son of God? Has the Son of God come forth into the earth as a bush in the desert?

He was not a bush, but He grew where only bushes grow. A different kind of plant, He was a tender suckling coming out of parched ground. From the beginning His life was in danger, so vulnerable, so helpless. Born in a stable, proclaimed to be the Messiah by an angelic host, He was immediately pursued by a wicked king who tried to take His life. He grew up in a carpenter's shop in an isolated village that the nation despised. After following His trade, He left the carpentry shop and went into the wilderness to meet a man called "John the Baptist." Following Jesus' baptism, the Spirit led Him into the desert for forty days. There in total isolation, Jesus met the tempter who came with old questions that every man in isolation has faced, "Who are You? Why are You here?" Origin and identity, and destiny and purpose, these are the issues of the wilderness. Maybe He is just a wanderer in the land of Nod who does not know who He is or where He is going. It is so easy for man to lose himself in isolation. He faced the pain of every wanderer since the time of Cain. Will His life be survival or will it be destiny?

The temptations came in a hot, barren place (Matthew 4:1-11). No one was near to help; it is a land without inhabitant. Like a bush in the desert, He stood alone. "If you are the Son of God, eat!" a voice spoke out. "You will die in this wilderness!" The tempter was right: a man could die in this desert. Restraining Himself, He stood resisting the temptation to save Himself. "If you are the Son of God, jump down!" the voice spoke again. "Show the world who you are; perform for them! You can do it; jump!" Did He really know who He was? Did He need to prove that to Himself and the world? Down deep inside He resolved that question once and for all; no matter what others thought or said, He was the Son of God, and He would not take things into His own hands and test the Father. "If you will fall down and worship me, the kingdoms of the earth will be yours!" the voice enticed Him. Here was His chance; He could now build His own kingdom and live for Himself. Surely the Father would understand and some day He would do the Father's will. Yet now...no, no, no! He could not! He refused to build His own kingdom and to save Himself; He settled it there. His purpose and destiny would be in doing the Father's will, even if He had to lay down His life. He broke the temptation to lawlessness; He was free!

He was not a bush, but the world considered Him a bush, for "He was despised and forsaken of men, a man of sorrows, and acquainted with grief; and like one from whom men hide their face, He was despised, and we did not esteem Him" (Isaiah 53:3). The pain of rejection was within Him. He understood the words of Job, "They are driven from the community; they shout against them as against a thief" (Job 30:5). He experienced the loneliness of the dreadful valleys. He could identify with those who dwell among the bushes; for He Himself said, "...The foxes have holes, and the birds of the air have nests; but the Son of Man has nowhere to lay His head" (Matthew 8:20). He knew the pain of those dwellers. People would call Him "Man of Sorrows." He Himself cried out in the night, alone. He knew the pain of rejection; He knew what it was to be despised, to have man consider Him as having no value. He knew what it was to face isolation and rejection.

The rejection was so intense at one time that He cried out, "But I am a worm, and not a man, a reproach of men, and despised by the people. All who see me sneer at me; they separate with the lip, they wag the head, saying, `Commit Thyself to the Lord; let Him deliver him; let Him rescue him, because He delights in him'" (Psalm 22:6-8). Lifted up in their midst, yet all alone; there was no one to comfort Him. He suffered in isolation. Who can know the depth of pain more than the man who suffers alone? In every way He experienced the alienation of man. How much less can a man be than to consider himself a worm? These words reflect the scorn of the people; they considered Him of no worth. Yet not for Himself did He endure the reproach of men; "Surely our griefs He Himself bore, and our sorrows He carried..." (Isaiah 53:4). He received our pain; He carried our sorrows; He entered into our isolation.

He Who experienced the isolation of rejection, was He a wanderer? No, Jesus did not live in isolation; He lived among men. He was not afraid to touch or be touched; He gathered His disciples around Him. They ate and slept with Him, walked with Him, and prayed with Him; He was open and transparent before men. He did not defend His reputation; the ill-reputed came near and He received them; even sinners came close to Him without fear. The multitudes came and He taught them and touched them; healing their sick He blessed them; He poured out His life for them. He did not live unto Himself; fear and insecurity did not bind Him. He knew Who He was and why He was here. He had purpose, He had destiny, He walked as the Son of God. His worth did not depend upon what He did. He was not a wanderer, nor was He a performer. Moved only by compassion, He never gave in to performance before man. He was in union with the Father, and He lived to do the Father's will. He had joined His heart to the Father; His will He had submitted to Him; He did not have to be in control. He was free to do the Father's will.

Hostility

"Crucify Him! Crucify Him!" The words came strong and clear from the hearts of the people. Those words expressed all the hatred and hostility since the time of Cain. All the anger of man, working wrath and hostility, burst forth like a storm upon the Son of God. From deep within the heart, dissensions, conflicts, and divisions surged upward like a torrent of many waters to destroy Him Who stood before them. A strong sectarian, religious spirit could not resist the opportunity to strike the Son of God. Violent spirits entered in; the people would not desist until they had spilled His blood upon the ground. Those words, "Crucify Him!" released and expressed the hostility of all men from Cain down through time. He at Whose birth angels announced "Peace on earth!" found no peace among men.

The alienation of man separated from man fell upon Him. "...The chastisement of our peace was upon him; and with His stripes we are healed" (Isaiah 53:5, KJV). The full expression of man's hostility fell upon Him, and having received it, He was able to bring forth peace through His cross. As one version puts it, "...the chastisment [needful to obtain] peace...was upon Him..." (Amplified Bible). The prophet prophesied, "And this One will be our peace..." (Micah 5:5). "...Having made peace through the blood of His cross..." (Colossians 1:20), He broke the walls of alienation separating man from God and man from man. Reconciliation with God brings reconciliation with men. Now one body and one Spirit make all men one in Christ. He became the fulfillment of His prayer, "Father, may they be one."

Peace confronted the hostility of man and overcame through forgiveness. "Father, forgive them!" (Luke 23:34), were the words spoken from the cross. Those words put to death all the hostility of man. It would go no further; there at the cross hostility fully vented itself and died. Then could Isaiah say, "...By His scourging we are healed..." (Isaiah 53:5). His blood, poured out upon the ground, "...speaks better than the blood of Abel" (Hebrews 12:24). Whereas, the blood of Abel cried out, "Vengeance!" the blood of Jesus cried out, "Peace! Peace!"

"And although you were formerly alienated and hostile in mind, engaged in evil deeds, yet He has now reconciled you in His fleshly body through death..." (Colossians 1:21,22). His death overcame the hostility of man.

Alienation

At last the death of alienation came upon the Son of God. The last words from the cross, "...My God, My God, why hast Thou forsaken Me?" (Mark 15:34), find the Son of God experiencing the first phase of alienation, separation from the Father. This separation has come in reverse to the order of alienation man experiences. He has come to the end of bearing the alienation of man. For Him Who had always lived in union with the Father, to experience for the first time alienation from the Father, caused Him pain far beyond anything man could know. In the depths of suffering, facing death, Jesus experienced the withdrawal of the love of the Father. The blackness of an eternity without God came upon Him. Even the earth became dark at noonday when He experienced the despair of man separated from God.

"He was pierced through for our transgressions, He was crushed for our iniquities; ...the Lord was pleased to crush Him, putting Him to grief; ...if He would render Himself as a guilt offering, ...He poured out Himself to death, and was numbered with the transgressors; yet He Himself bore the sin of many" (Isaiah 53:5,10,12). The Father laid upon Him all the darkness of man's sin. He Who had lived without defilement, now experienced defilement. His soul was crushed under the weight of man's sin. He died as a sinner!

He hanged upon a tree, naked and exposed to the world. The curse of man's sin was upon Him, "...for he who is hanged is accursed of God..." (Deuteronomy 21:23). God now put the shame and guilt that came upon man in the Garden upon the sinless One. There was nothing to cover His nakedness, not even an apron of fig leaves. The guilt and shame that every sinner has carried, now is brought before the whole world. Having no place to hide, with nothing with which to cover Himself, the Son of Man now bears the guilt. The behavior of hiding and covering oneself was not found in the Son of God during all the days of His life, nor could He hide at death. He was transparent before man and God. Guiltless, shameless, He was free from fear. People could come close; anyone could look upon Him. He made the way for every man to be free of his fig leaves. No longer does man have to live hiding and covering himself. He lifted the shame and guilt from man. Blessed is the man who can say, "...He has clothed me with garments of salvation, He has wrapped me with a robe of righteousness..." (Isaiah 61:10).

The Son of God experienced the alienation of man. To the last drop He drank from the cup until there was nothing left. Now those who drink from the same cup find healing, deliverance, and salvation. Listen to the words of Jesus:

> The Spirit of the Lord God is upon me,
> Because the Lord has anointed me
> To bring good news to the afflicted;
> He has sent me to bind up the brokenhearted,
> To proclaim liberty to captives,
> And freedom to prisoners;
> To proclaim the favorable year of the Lord,
> And the day of vengeance of our God;
> To comfort all who mourn,
> To grant those who mourn in Zion,
> Giving them a garland instead of ashes,
> The oil of gladness instead of mourning,
> The mantle of praise instead of a spirit of fainting,
> So they will be called oaks of righteousness,
> The planting of the Lord, that He may be glorified.
>   Isaiah 61:1-3

Study/Discussion Guide

PRACTICAL APPLICATION

Chapter One: *Society in Trouble*

1. **Cultural Isolation.** "The problem of despair and hopelessness is a phenomenon of the twentieth century. People have become alienated within their own culture" (p.l).

   a. What has caused this sense of despair and hopelessness with our culture?

   b. Do you have a tendency toward hopeless and despair? Describe some of the struggles you experience.

   c. Pray and ask God to show you the roots of this problem.

2. **Life Support Structures.** "All life support structures have deteriorated within our society...Basically there are three substructures of society: family, church, and civil government. These three furnish a covering of protection in which life grows" (p.2).

   a. Describe your view of the life support structures of society. Do you see them intact and functioning?

   b. Have you experienced a broken family relationship? How has this affected you?

   c. Do you experience community within and without the church? How would you describe your relationships? Do you feel bonded to others, or are you isolated as a person?

    d.   Do you feel secure or insecure in the governmental system of your nation? What are some of your greater concerns? Do you have hope?

    e.   Have you built walls of isolation about yourself?

    f.   Does life have meaning and purpose for you?

Note: These questions expose pain and fear within. Please, do not stop at this point. Take heart and allow God to release new life in you. There is hope; there is healing.

3. **Like A Bush In The Desert.** Please read Jeremiah 17:5-8.

    a.   Look at the cover of the book and describe what you see.

    b.   In what ways does your life compare to a bush in the desert?

    c.   Do you believe God can make you a tree planted by the waters?

    d.   Contrast the bush and the tree. What makes the difference between the two?

Note: Within the following chapters you will find principles of truth that will set you free. It is never too late. Believe God for a new beginning.

Behold, I will do something new,
Now it will spring forth;
Will you not be aware of it?
I will even make a roadway in the wilderness,
Rivers in the desert.
Isaiah 43:18

Chapter Two: *Guilt, Shame, and Fear*

1. **Hiding and Covering.** "The day man transgressed and broke covenant with God, he became a hiding, covering creature" (p.4). Read Genesis 3:7-10.

    a. What are the basic problems of man presented in verse 10?

    b. How would you describe guilt and shame?

    c. How do you see fear working together with guilt and shame?

2. **A Mental Processing of Guilt.** "Following the pattern of the first man who put the blame upon the woman, men still try to maintain innocence through denial and blame" (p.4). Describe three ways man processes guilt:

    a.

    b.

    c.

3. **The Entrance of Evil.** "Guilt is more than a mental or psychological problem. It has deep spiritual roots. It involves the problem of evil" (p.4).

    a. What does evil do when it enters the soul of man?

    b. Where does shame come from?

    c. Discuss shame in relationship to evil. Describe the sense of nakedness that comes with evil.

4. **Dealing with Nakedness.** "Man in his attempt to deal with guilt makes a choice, either to cover with a religious covering or to accept nakedness as normal (p.5).

    a. How does one recognize a religious covering? Discuss the fig-leaf covering.

    b. What is God's answer for guilt and shame?

c.   What kind of covering have you used to hide guilt and shame?

5.   **Personal Application for the Woman:** Perhaps you are struggling with bondages of fear and lust. When evil is experienced in the time of innocence, fear and guilt can keep you from freedom in the marriage relationship. Strongholds of fear and perversion can be broken. How did the Lord wash away the filth of the daughters of Zion? He cleansed them "...by the Spirit of judgment and the Spirit of burning" (Isaiah 4:4). The Holy Spirit is a fire that cleanses from all defilement. "...And He Himself will baptize you with the Holy Spirit and fire" (Matthew 3:11). God by His Spirit is able to set you free from fear and guilt. That which man has defiled, God can cleanse. You can be clean!

Chapter Three: *Hostility*

1.   **Without Peace.** "Since the time of the fall, hostility as a basic behavior has dominated man's history. Conflict and division, anger and hatred, conquering and subduing, describe this behavior. Why has he not been able to live in peace" (p.8)?

a.   Give two main reasons why there has been no peace in the history of man.

b.   Discuss these two problems within society today.

c.   Share your own struggles in these two areas.

d.   How do the deeds of the flesh described in Galatians 5:20, fit into this problem?

2.   **Without Union.** "Man has a basic need for community. Whether it be from the need of security or for union, man was not created to dwell alone...Brotherhood is a basic need within man because God created him His own image. Within God there is no alienation"(p.9).

a.   Discuss the Trinity of God in regard to union and alienation.

b.   What are the two principles that work life and death in man?

c. How do we know we have passed from death into life? Read I John 3:11-14.

d. Do you believe the prayer of Jesus will be answered today among men? Read John 17:21-23.

Chapter Four: *Bitterness and Unforgiveness*

1. **Man Separated from Man.** "Pain that is suppressed will come out in destructive ways: anger and hostility, blame and criticism, rebellion and violence. Time does not cause it to go away" (p.12).

    a. Explain why alienation causes the deepest pain within man.

    b. List the relationships in which alienation has prevailed. How would you describe the pain coming out of these relationships?

2. **The Pain Inside.** "Pain held inside can create conditions of chronic sadness and depression, fear and isolation, self-punishment and suicide, addictions and addictive behavior" (p.12).

    a. Have you experienced pain? Describe the cause.

    b. What effect has it had upon you?

3. **Abandoned by God.** "The pain grows deeper when one feels God has abandoned him. Many struggle with the question, Where is God when it hurts?" (p.12).

    a. Have you struggled with the above question?

    b. What are the losses and disappointments in life that have caused you to be bitter toward God?

    c. Do you believe God is the author of evil?

Note: The working of evil does three things:
(a. Destorts the image of God.
(b. Destroys faith in God.
(c. Separates man from God.

4.   **Bitterness.** "Out of a wounded spirit a destructive behavior comes forth. What is more destructive than bitterness? Bitterness is a root that grows deep within the soul, and whose fruit is death. It is the cancer of the soul..." (p.13).

   a.   Describe bitterness as a root growing within the soul. Read Hebrews 12:12-15.

   b.   What are the consequences of bitterness?

   c.   Explain bitterness working pain within the emotions.

   d.   Do you see any patterns of bitterness in your life? Describe these patterns.

5.   **Forgiveness.** "Forgiveness is the key to releasing pain and receiving healing. A principle of the Kingdom is found in Luke 6:37, `...Pardon, and you will be pardoned'" (p.14).

   a.   Does time cause the pain to go away?

   b.   How do the Scriptures teach you to release pain?

   c.   What is forgiveness? Read Matthew 18:21-35.

   d.   What are the principles of the Kingdom in regards to forgiveness? Read Matthew 6:12,14,15.

Note: Forgiveness basically means to release another from debt. To forgive means to pardon a debt. This comes as an act of the will rather than a release of the emotions. You choose to forgive, the feelings come later. Three things to remember:
(a. Forgiveness is a choice, not a feeling.
(b. Forgiveness chooses to love and not hate.
(c. By forgiving one releases the person and cancels the debt.

Note: Forgiveness releases God.
  (a. Forgiveness releases God's forgiveness for you.
     Read Matthew 6:14,15; Mark 11:23-25.
  (b. Forgiveness releases God's forgiveness to others.
     Read Matthew 18:18.
  (c. Forgiveness releases God's healing in you.
     Read Luke 6:37.

Practical Application: List the persons you need to forgive. Be specific as to what you need to release. As you release others, you yourself will be released.

Chapter Five: *Isolation*

1. **Rejected Brotherhood.** "When he [Cain] rejected brotherhood, he became a wanderer and vagrant in the earth. He could nowhere be at rest for he dwelt in the land of Nod, the land of restlessness" (p.15).

   a. What two things confront man in his isolation?

   b. When Cain cried out, "My pain is too great to bear!" what did he experience?

   c. What are three things man loses when he rejects brotherhood?

   d. How are these three things vital to man's life?

2. **Man Separated from Himself.** "One comes to see the frightening results of alienation. In isolation man loses perspective. Man does not find himself by looking within himself; neither does he find purpose by living for himself. When he no longer can see the face of God, man loses all perspective" (p.16).

   a. What is the line that separates man from the rest of the animals in the world?

b. What two questions does man ask in his search for uniqueness and purpose?

c. Do you see in man's history an upward progression or a downward spiral?

3. **Modern-Day Wanderers.** "Job describes a generation living in isolation. The scenario of a people living in a wilderness describes the emotional and spiritual conditions of a generation alienated from itself" (p.16).

a. Read Job 30:5-8, and describe the generation Job saw.

b. Compare these conditions to our day.

4. **Addictive Behavior.** "Isolation is the number-one problem in this society. The breakdown of the family and the lack of brotherhood in the community has left a generation living in a vacuum of emotional needs. Without union, without bonding, they live in emptiness and spaciousness. Without purpose and meaning in life...This generation has lost its way; it has been born in an addictive culture" (p.18).

a. What are the roots of the culture that produce addictive behavior?

b. What are the basic needs of the addict?

Note: Full recovery for the addict encompasses two stages: first, abstain from the compulsion; second, deal with the underlying issues causing the compulsions.

a. In order to release grace in his life, he must come to a point of truth and honesty. The pattern of denial must be broken. He must come to face himself as he is, and he must face God with all his guilt and shame. This is the point that grace is release and addiction is broken. This is the point of righteousness.

b. In order to experience union, he must release control of his life. Addiction represents an attempt to assert control over one's life. To release control means one submits his will and joins his heart to God. Without this action one will not have the union with God that is necessary to fill the emptiness and find purpose. The issue of rebellion and lawlessness must be faced.

c. In order to be healed, he must touch the pain in his life. Pain does not go away through denial. Pain can be released and grieved out by taking three steps:

    (a. Break denial and repression by facing the pain.

    (b. Share the pain with God in prayer. Cry it out, or shout it out.

    (c. Share the pain with others.

    (d. Remember, peace comes through reconciliation. Forgive and take responsibility for your actions.

Chapter Six: *The Performer*

1. **The Search for Significance.** "A culture filled with isolation will give priority to performance and success. Man will begin a search for significance" (p.20).

    a. Did Cain remain in isolation? Read Genesis 4:16,17.

    b. What are two extreme behaviors coming out of isolation?

    c. Do you know people who fit into both categories?

    d. How have you been affected by isolation and loneliness?

2. **The Kingdom of Self.** "Succes means self-worth, significance, and purpose in life. Whatever it takes, he will put out the effort to reach his goals. So he enters into a mode of performance that will produce for him all the things he desires. What comes forth is the kingdom of self" (p.21).

    a. Can you describe the kingdom of self?

    b. Can you describe the man who is driven to perform?

3. **An Idol of the Heart.** "Inside the man a certain pride comes that isolates him further. He has built an image for himself from his performance. Success has created an image of worth. He dedicates his whole life to creating and maintaining this image" (p.21).

    a. What kind of image does man build for himself out of performance?

b. Would you consider this image as an idol of the heart? Read Ezekiel 14:3.

c. How would you describe this person at work?

d. How would you describe this person at home? Children? Wife?

e. Discuss the family relationship built around performance?

4. **Addictive Behavior.** "The performer's drive to excel will carry him right into addictive behavior" (p.22). Using the same basic needs of the addict, discuss the needs of the performer:

a. The need to suspend time

b. The need to be invincible

c. The need to become immortal

5. **The Performer as a Machine.** "A basic question every man asks himself is, `Can I produce enough to be successful?' In a society where isolation is prevalent, the focus of attention will be given to success and performance. Success becomes the purpose for life. In the process man becomes a machine whose sole purpose becomes production" (p.23).

a. What is the purpose of a machine?

b. What happens to machines when they no longer can produce?

c. How can modern man be productive and useful without becoming a machine?

d. What really gives purpose and value to life?

e. Discuss the words of Jesus, "He who keeps his life for himself shall lose it, but he who gives his life shall find it" (Matthew 10:39, paraphrased).

Chapter Seven: *Lawlessness*

1. **The Enigma of This Age.** "This decline is the enigma of this age. Man has not learned to govern himself because he is still living in lawlessness as an individual...Ultimately, alienation will reject authority, refuse restraint, and give itself to lawlessness" (p.25).

   a. Has man's great technological development solved the problems of society?

   b. What two problems accompanied the development of Cain's society?

   c. How would you describe a humanistic society?

   d. What parallel can you draw between our society and the society of Cain?

2. **The Alienation of Father's Hearts.** "A phenomenon of the Twentieth Century is the alienation of fathers' hearts from their children. At no other time in history do we find the union between father and children destroyed by its culture" (p.25).

   a. What in our society has caused the hearts of the fathers to be turned away from the children?

   b. What do you think is the curse that is prophised by Malachi by prophet? Read Malachi 4:5,6.

   c. Describe the effect within society of:

      (a. Violence
      (b. Insanity
      (c. Hedonism

3. **The Nature of Rebellion.** "...rebellion within the human soul alienates man from God and man from man. One sees the nature or working of rebellion within in three ways: it refuses to bend its will, it refuses to give its heart, and it refuses to release control" (p.26).

   a. How would you describe a person will a bent will?

b. When one is unable to give his heart, how does this affect his relationship to God? To others? Read Matthew 15:8,9.

c. Is control an issue with God? How does it affect one's relationship to God?

d. Have you struggled in the above areas? Share the experiences that brought you release.

e. Have you found peace and rest in your life? Discuss the life of the wicked from Isaiah 57:20,21.

4. **A Declaration of Independence.** "Many addictions enslave man as he makes his declaration of independence. The bottom line is this: when one rejects authority the body rules over man" (p.27).

a. What are areas of lust by which you are enslaved?

b. Did you reject your father's authority?

c. Have you ever submitted to any authority?

Note: A time of repentance allows God's grace to penetrate these areas of lust. To the depth of repentance, to that level grace will come. Without the grace of God there can be no freedom. Repentance releases the intervention of God's grace.

Note: In dealing with other problems coming out of rebellion, there is an order of righteousness that brings order into one's life. It is the order of righteousness that brings life and sustains life. Become a seeker of His Kingdom and His righteousness (Matthew 6:33).

Chapter Eight: *A Righteous Man*

1. **A Righteous Man with a Father's Heart.** "Noah was a father with a father's heart. No alienation separated him from his sons. They had his heart and he had their hearts., They stood together in a critical time; they were united because their hearts were bonded" (p.29).

    a. What is the first key in bringing sons into the ark?

    b. Describe children who have never had their father's heart. What causes them to conform to their culture and friends?

    c. Why were Noah's sons strong men?

    d. What is the most valuable gift a father give to his sons and daughters?

2. **A Righteous Man with a Father's Authority.** "An essential function of authority is the formation of character. Through the imposition of discipline, we form character. Discipline is a process of training that develops self-control, endurance, and good behavior" (p.30).

    a. What is the second key in bringing sons into the ark?

    b. What is formed under a father's authority?

    c. Compare the formation of clay in the hand of the potter to the formation of a father's authority.

    d. Discuss the working of authority through discipline, endurance, and obedience. Is there formation of character without authority?

    e. List character traits that are essential to rightousness. How would you form each of these in your children?

3. **The Function of Authority.** "A father should be `...like a refuge from the wind, and a shelter from the storm, like streams of water in a dry country, like the shade of a huge rock in a parched land'" (Isaiah 32:2).

    a. Read Isaiah 32:1-7, describe the righteous man.

    b. List and discuss the purposes of authority.

   c.   Describe children who have not submitted to the discipline of learning. Read verses 3-5.

   d.   What is the result when righteousness is formed in children? Read verse 17.

   e.   What kind of home will you have when the order of righteousness is established? Read verse 18.

Chapter Nine: *God the Father*

1   **Sitting on a Throne.** "The struggle with the father image of God centers around authority. For some, to envision God as sitting on a throne brings a response of consternation at His being tyrannical, arbitrary, and despotic. For them authority is contrary to the exercise of free will, subjecting them to absolutes of another world" (p.32).

   a.   Why does God sit on a throne?

   b.   What accompanies His authority at the throne? Read Psalm 89:14.

   c.   How do the titles "our Father...our Potter" describe the twofold relationship of God to His children? Read Isaiah 64:8.

2.   **A Spirit of Sonship or a Spirit of Slavery.** "What is the cry from your heart? Have you ever known a father's love? Have you ever submitted to a father's authority? Perhaps there is only fear and distrust, or maybe there is resistance and rebellion. Many live under a spirit of slavery because they have never known a father's heart" (p.33).

   a.   How would you answer the above question?

   b.   How would you describe your father relationship?

   c.   What would you list as positive qualities of a father image?

   d.   How would you compare the slave to a son? What factors make the relationship different?

e. Describe three qualities of sonship from II Timothy 1:7.

3. **Without Alienation.** "The heart of the Father is without alienation" (p.35).

    a. What does the parable of the Prodigal Son mean to you?

    b. Discuss the Father's heart revealed by this parable.

Chapter Ten: *Like A Bush In The Desert*

1. **Like a Bush in the Desert.** "For He grew up before Him like a tender shoot, and like a root out of parched ground; He has no stately form or majesty that we should look upon Him, nor appearance that we should be attracted to Him" (Isaiah 53:2).

    a. Who is this that comes up out of parched ground?

    b. Who is this whose form is not stately or majestic, whose appearance is without beauty to create desire?

    c. Was Jesus a bush? Why was He planted where only bushes grow?

    d. Describe the condition in which Jesus came into the world.

2. **The Pain of Rejection.** "'He was despised and forsaken of men, a man of sorrows, and acquainted with grief; and like from whom men hide their face He was despised, and we did not esteem Him' (Isaiah 53:3). The pain of rejection was with Him" (p.37).

    a. Did Jesus know what it was to be despised, to have men consider Him as having no value? Explain.

    b. How did Jesus feel when the people scorned him?
        Read Psalm 22:6-8.

    c. Was Jesus an isolated person?

    d. Why was He rejected if all He did was good? Read Isaiah 54:4.

e. What are the rejections in your life that were carried by Jesus?

3. **Hostility.** "` Crucify Him! Crucify Him!'...Those words express all the hatred and hostility since the time of Cain" (p.38).

    a. How would you explain the hostility of men toward Jesus?

    b. Was there hostility within Jesus toward men?

    c. What hostility in your life was laid upon Him?

    d. How did Jesus confront the hostility of man? What were the words that broke the hostility of man?

4. **Alienation.** "At last the death of alienation came upon the Son of God. The last words from the cross, ` My God, My God, why hast Thou forsaken Me?' find the Son of God experiencing the first phase of alienation, separation from the Father" (p.39).

    a. Did Jesus lose union with the Father?

    b. What was put upon Him that broke this union?

    c. What sins, guilt, and shame from your life were put upon Him?

    d. Are you still carrying guilt and shame? Read II Corinthians 7:1.

    Note: Discuss Isaiah 53, and compare it to Isaiah 61:1-3. Allow the ministry and work of these chapters to come forth in your life.